JOYFUL EASTER

Rediscovering Hymns of Praise for Easter and Lent

HYMN HISTORIES AND STORIES
40 DEVOTIONALS FOR LENT
BIBLE PASSAGES AND PRAYERS

JOHN WILLIAMSON

POLMARRON PRESS

An independent Publisher bringing you books everyone will want to read.

We like being small, this means our fantastic writers and editors can create the books they love and you will want to read. Our focus is non-fiction, and you'll find our books in both paperback and eBook formats. We've got a book club too, join below (dogs welcome).

Content Disclaimer: The hymns contained within this book are in the public domain and are freely accessible to the general public. However, other content in this book is protected by copyright and may not be reproduced, duplicated, or transmitted without direct written permission from the author or the publisher. Under no circumstances will any blame or legal responsibility be held against the publisher or author for any damages, reparation, or monetary loss due to the information contained within this book, either directly or indirectly. Legal Notice: This book contains a compilation of hymns that are in the public domain, allowing readers to freely access, reproduce, and share these specific materials. However, other content within this book is protected by copyright. It is intended for personal use, and readers are not permitted to amend, distribute, sell, use, quote, or paraphrase any part of the copyrighted content without obtaining explicit consent from the author or publisher. Disclaimer Notice: Please note that the hymns included in this document are in the public domain, while other content is protected by copyright. This book is provided for educational and entertainment purposes only. Every effort has been made to present accurate, up-to-date, reliable, and complete information. The opinions and views presented in this book are those of the author, reflecting their personal beliefs and interpretations.

No warranties of any kind, whether declared or implied, are associated with the copyrighted content. Readers acknowledge that the author is not engaged in the rendering of legal, financial, medical, or professional advice. The content within this book, excluding the hymns in the public domain, has been created by the author and is protected by copyright. By reading this document, the reader agrees that under no circumstances is the author responsible for any losses, direct or indirect, incurred as a result of the use of the copyrighted information contained within this document, including, but not limited to, errors, omissions, or inaccuracies.

© Copyright Polmarron Press 2023 - All rights reserved.
www.polmarronpress.com

Joyful Easter

Rediscovering Hymns
of Praise for Easter and Lent
25 Hymn Histories and Stories
40 Devotionals for Lent
Bible Passages and Prayers

CONTENTS   Page

Welcome	5
Introduction	6
Lent	8
40 Days of Reflection	9
1. Forty Days and Forty Nights	15
2. Lord, Who Throughout These Forty Days	19
3. Alas! And Did My Saviour Bleed?	22
4. O Sacred Head, Now Wounded	25
5. Lead Me To Calvary	29
6. When I Survey The Wondrous Cross	33
7. The Strife is O'er, the Battle Done	36
8. What Wondrous Love Is This	40
9. Ah, Holy Jesus, How Hast Thou Offended	43
10. Go To Dark Gethsemane	47
Easter	51
11. Christ the Lord is Risen Today	52
12. He Is Risen, He Is Risen!	56
13. Up from the Grave He Arose	60
14. Thine Be the Glory	63
15. Jesus Christ is Risen Today	66
16. The Day of Resurrection	69
17. I Know That My Redeemer Lives	72
18. Welcome, Happy Morning	76
19. Alleluia, Sing to Jesus	81
20. Low in the Grave He Lay	85
21. All Glory, Laud, and Honour	89
22. Crown Him with Many Crowns	93
23. Love Divine, All Loves Excelling	97
24. Now Thank We All Our God	100
25. Praise to the Lord, the Almighty	104
A joyful Easter to you!	107
Also by Polmarron Press	108

Welcome

There's a profound resonance in the words of St. Augustine, "He who sings prays twice." This sentiment captures the heart of this book exploring the rich tapestry of hymns that have been woven into the fabric of Easter and Lent through time. In the chapters that follow, you'll uncover the lyrical beauty and spiritual depth of 25 carefully selected hymns of praise for the season. These are not just songs; they are prayers set to music, echoing through centuries and carrying with them stories of faith, hope, and redemption. You'll be introduced to the authors behind them - ordinary men and women who were moved to express their extraordinary faith in verse. Their biographies are as varied as their hymns, yet, they all share a common thread. A deep love for Christ and a desire to express it through their words accessible by all.

Each hymn carries within its lyrics a story waiting to be told. Some speak of Christ's sacrifice on the cross; others rejoice in His resurrection. Still others plead for mercy or express a longing for His presence. These stories will be unraveled for you to understand and enjoy. But this exploration doesn't stop at hymns. You will also find 40 prayers specifically crafted for the season of Lent. These daily devotionals and moments of reflection are designed to guide you through your own spiritual journey during this sacred time.

In addition, you'll discover relevant Bible passages that shed light on the themes explored in each hymn and prayer. These passages serve as signposts along your path, illuminating your understanding and enriching your worship experience.
 Finally, there will be devotionals and personal prayers interspersed throughout these pages. They serve as quiet interludes for reflection and personal communion with God that will stir your soul, challenge your faith, and ultimately, draw you closer to the One who is the reason for our songs and prayers.So here we are. No fanfare, no grand introductions. Just a simple invitation to step into the hymns of praise that have shaped the worship experience of people throughout centuries during Easter and Lent.

Introduction

The season of Easter and Lent is an exceptional time for Christians around the world. It's a period of reflection, penitence, and celebration, marking Jesus Christ's journey from his crucifixion to his glorious resurrection. One way we can engage with this profound narrative is through hymns – songs that encapsulate our faith and articulate our devotion.

Hymns are powerful tools for worship that connect us with God and help us reflect on Jesus' journey during Easter and Lent. These sacred songs have been used throughout history as expressions of praise, prayer, and teaching.

They serve as a conduit for connecting our hearts to God's heart in ways words alone cannot achieve. When sung in congregation or solitude, or simply read as prayers, they create a spiritual atmosphere conducive to divine encounters.

Hymns not only enhance our worship experience but also serve as weapons against spiritual adversaries. The harmonious blend of music and lyrics filled with biblical truths can dispel darkness and usher in God's light into our lives.

Singing hymns together as we often do, holds an emotional and spiritual. Many studies have found that group singing can foster feelings of social connectedness and shared purpose - elements crucial during Easter when people unite to commemorate Christ's sacrifice on the cross.

As we look further into these hymns over this period, it will be more than just learning their melodies or reciting their lyrics - it will be about understanding their origins too. Knowing who wrote them and why gives us a richer appreciation for these works and enhances our connection with them.

If you encounter difficulties grasping some hymn meanings or struggle with some melodies remember this; It's not about perfection but connection. Sing from your heart; your sincerity is more important than hitting the right notes.

Here are some points of guidance for you as you travel through this book:

Psalm 96:1

"Sing to the Lord a new song; sing to the Lord, all the earth."

Steps to Take:

1. Engage with the hymns: Don't just sing, meditate on the lyrics and their meanings.
2. Learn about the authors: Understanding their experiences can give you a deeper connection to the hymn.

3. Pray before singing: Ask God to open your heart and mind to receive His message through each hymn.

Important Takeaways:

- Hymns are powerful tools for worship that connect us with God's heart.

- They hold spiritual and emotional power capable of driving away adversarial forces.

- Group singing fosters feelings of social connectedness and shared purpose.

- It's not about perfection but connection when it comes to singing hymns; sincerity is key.

I hope you enjoy exploring 25 Hymns of Praise for Easter and Lent as you delve into their history, learn about their authors, understand their context, appreciate their lyrics, and ultimately use them as instruments of worship during this sacred season.

Lent

As we enter the solemn season of Lent - a sacred journey of penance, reflection, and preparation spanning the six weeks leading up to Easter begins. Like the 40 days Jesus spent fasting in the desert before embarking on his public ministry, Lent's duration, approximately 40 days, carries a symbolic weight, inviting us to walk alongside Christ in our own introspective pilgrimage.

Lent commences on Ash Wednesday, a day of humility and reflection, and gracefully concludes on Holy Saturday, the eve of Easter Sunday. These dates, ever-shifting on the lunar calendar, usher us into a period where we can engage in spiritual practices as acts of repentance and self-discipline.

On Ash Wednesday, the tangible symbols of repentance are etched onto foreheads - ashes made from the burnt palms of the previous year's Palm Sunday, forming a cross. This simple yet profound act serves as a visual reminder of our mortality and a beckoning call to repentance. It marks the initiation of Lent, a season not of despair but of hope, where self-denial and spiritual discipline become the compass guiding our hearts.

Many, during these 40 days, choose to relinquish certain luxuries or habits as a voluntary surrender echoing Jesus' journey in the desert. This intentional act of self-denial is not a mere ritual; it's a deliberate alignment with the Lenten spirit in preparation for the joyous celebration that awaits.

This 40-day pilgrimage offers a sacred space for self-examination, a dedicated time for self-discipline, and a focused pursuit of spiritual growth. Lent is not a solitary venture but a communal experience, an invitation to join the countless believers worldwide in preparing for the grand celebration of Easter; the momentous resurrection of Jesus Christ. A celebration that echoes with the proclamation: He is risen!

May this Lenten journey prepare your hearts to fully embrace the joy and transformative power of Easter.

40 Days of Reflection

During Lent take time each day to reflect using these daily devotions.

Day 1: Start a Gratitude Journal

Write down three things you're thankful for each day during Lent. It will help shift your focus from what's lacking to the abundance in your life.

Day 2: Embrace Forgiveness

Consider those you need to forgive and seek forgiveness from. Let go of grudges, knowing that God's forgiveness is boundless.

Day 3: Prioritise Prayer

In the busyness of life, make time for prayer today. Speak to God as a friend, sharing your joys and concerns. Open your heart and listen for His guidance. Prayer is a conversation; make it a priority.

Day 4: Acts of Kindness

Perform a small act of kindness for someone today. It could be a word of encouragement, a helping hand, or a thoughtful gesture. Reflect on how these acts can reflect Christ's love.

Day 5: Fasting from Distractions

Consider fasting from a distraction today - maybe social media, excessive TV, or a bad habit, and use this time to be present with Him.

Day 6: Reflect on Humility

Reflect on humility today. Think of areas in your life where humility can be found. Remember that Jesus, in all His glory, demonstrated humility.

Day 7: Reflect on Renewal

Just as spring brings new life to the earth, let this season renew your spirit.

Today, take a moment to reflect on the renewal Lent brings. Pray for a fresh start and the strength to grow in your faith.

Day 8: Seek Healing

Seek spiritual and emotional healing today. Identify areas that need healing and ask God for His restoring touch. Remember, healing is a journey, and God is with you every step.

Day 9: Surrender Control

Surrender control to God by acknowledging that you are not in control of everything. Let go of worry and trust that God is guiding your path. Pray for the strength to surrender.

Day 10: Acts of Service

Engage in an act of service today. Offer your time or skills to help someone in need. Reflect on how serving others reflects the sacrificial love of Jesus.

Day 11: Reflect on Repentance

Acknowledge your shortcomings and ask God for forgiveness. Repentance is a step towards a renewed and restored relationship with Him.

Day 12: Connect with Community

If it has been a while re-connect with your faith community. Attend a service, join a study group, or simply reach out to fellow believers. Community strengthens and supports our journey of faith.

Day 13: Gratitude for Creation

Express gratitude for God's creation today. Take a walk to enjoy nature and marvel at the beauty around you, and your place in God's glorious creation.

Day 14: Extend Grace

Remember the grace God extends to you daily and extend this grace to someone who may have wronged you. Pray for a heart that mirrors His grace towards others.

Day 15: Reflect on the Cross

Consider the sacrifice of Jesus and the depth of God's love. Ponder how the significance of the cross shapes your life and decisions.

Day 16: Patience in Waiting

Reflect on God's timing in your life and practice patience today. Trust that His plans are unfolding, even if the journey seems slow. Be patient and faithful.

Day 17: Share Your Faith Story

It doesn't have to be grand; it could be a simple conversation about what God means to you. Share your faith story with someone and let your light shine.

Day 18: Acts of Reparation

Consider acts of reparation. Is there someone you need to reconcile with? Take steps to mend broken relationships and seek forgiveness.

Day 19: Simplicity

Embrace simplicity today. Declutter your physical and mental space. Simplifying your life allows room for spiritual clarity and a deeper connection with God.

Day 20: Reflect on God's Love

Seek out and meditate on scriptures and bible passages that speak of His love. Allow this awareness to guide your interactions with others.

Day 21: Pray for Wisdom

Seek God's guidance in decisions big and small by praying for wisdom. Remember that God's wisdom surpasses human understanding.

Day 22: Compassion for Others
Cultivate compassion today. Walk in empathy with others recognising the struggles and joys of those around you and pray for a heart that mirrors Christ's compassion.

Day 23: Forgiveness for Yourself

Remember that God's forgiveness is complete and forgive yourself for past mistakes. Use this day to release guilt and shame, embracing the freedom found in Christ.

Day 24: Contemplate the Last Supper

Consider the significance of the last supper as a reminder of self-sacrifice, gratitude, and spiritual nourishment. Remember Jesus' sacrifice and the unity it brings to believers.

Day 25: Reflect on the Resurrection

Consider the hope it brings and the victory over sin and death. Praise God for the promise of new life in Christ.

Day 26: Engage in Acts of Reconciliation

If there are strained relationships in your life take steps toward reconciliation and peace. Reflect on God's call to be peacemakers.

Day 27: Pray for Strength

Whatever challenges you face, ask God for the strength to endure and the courage to overcome them. Trust that He is your source of strength.

Day 28: Gratitude for Relationships

Today express gratitude for the people and relationships in your life. Thank God for family, friends, co-workers and community and consider how these relationships reflect God's love and support.

Day 29: Reflect on Jesus' Compassion for the Marginalised

Consider how you can extend compassion to those who may be overlooked or in need.

Day 30: Simplicity in Speech

Practice speaking with kindness and honesty today. Let your words reflect the love and grace you've received from God.

Day 31: Seek Guidance in Scripture

Choose a passage that reflects or speaks to your current situation and meditate on its wisdom. Allow God's Word to guide your steps.

Day 32: Engage in Acts of Generosity today.

Share your resources with those in need and reflect on how God's generosity inspires you to be generous with others.

Day 33: Reflection on Humility

Acknowledge areas where humility can deepen your relationships. Remember that Jesus, in His humility, served others.

Day 34: Express Gratitude for Challenges

See challenges in your life as opportunities for growth and reliance on God. Pray for the strength and wisdom to navigate and face them.

Day 35: Prayer for Patience

Whether facing a difficult situation or a moment of frustration, seek God's grace to be patient with a short prayer. Remember that God's timing is perfect.

Day 36: Acts of Kindness

Engage in intentional acts of kindness today. Look for opportunities to brighten someone's day and reflect on the impact small gestures can have.

Day 37: Reflect on God's Provision

Consider God's provision in your life and His faithfulness in meeting your needs. Pray for a heart of gratitude and trust in His steadfastness.

Day 38: Gratitude for Jesus' Sacrifice on the Cross

Remember the depth of His love and the forgiveness made possible through His sacrifice.

Day 39: Reflect on God's Presence

Whether in moments of joy or sorrow, acknowledge that God is with you. Pray for an awareness of His constant presence today and every day.

Day 40: Easter Sunday

Celebrate the resurrection of Jesus today! Rejoice in the victory over sin and death. Thank God for the new life and hope found in Christ.

1
Forty Days and Forty Nights
George Hung Smyttan

Forty days and forty nights
You were fasting in the wild;
Forty days and forty nights
Tempted, and yet undefiled.

Shall not we your sorrow share
And from worldly joys abstain,
Fasting with unceasing prayer,
Strong with you to suffer pain?

Then if Satan on us press,
Flesh or spirit to assail,
Victor in the wilderness,
Grant we may not faint nor fail!

So shall we have peace divine;
Holier gladness ours shall be;
Round us, too, shall angels shine,
Such as served You faithfully.

Keep, O keep us, Savior dear,
Ever constant by your side,
That with you we may appear
At th'eternal Eastertide.

> Saints before the altar bending,
> Watching long in hope and fear,
> Suddenly the Lord, descending,
> In His temple shall appear:
> Come and worship,
> Come and worship,
> Worship Christ, the newborn King!

Authorship

George Hunt Smyttan (1822–1870) an Anglican clergyman, wrote "Forty Days and Forty Nights" in 1856. Born in the 19th century, Smyttan distinguished himself as a notable hymn writer, contributing significantly to Christian worship. Notably, he is recognised for his hymn "Forty Days and Forty Nights," a composition that has become integral to congregational singing worldwide. The hymn is inspired by the biblical account of Jesus' 40 days of fasting and temptation in the wilderness. It is commonly sung during the season of Lent, serving as a reflection on Christ's spiritual preparation for his public ministry.

Born into an era marked by rich hymnody, Smyttan's lyrical craftsmanship and religious depth are evident in this hymn, which reflects on the significance of the 40 days of Lent. The enduring resonance of "Forty Days and Forty Nights" underscores his ability to capture the essence of faith and convey it with eloquence. Beyond his hymn-writing contributions, Smyttan's creative work continues to impact the spiritual expression of communities.

The story within the hymn

"Forty Days and Forty Nights" reflects on the spiritual significance of this period, emphasising themes of self-discipline, temptation, and preparation for ministry. This beautiful hymn captures the essence of Jesus' 40 days in the wilderness, as described in the Gospels. It begins by recounting the period of His fasting in the wild, emphasising both the duration and the purity of His resolve against temptation.

By asking a poignant question the hymn invites us to consider sharing in

Jesus' sorrow and abstaining from worldly joys during the Lenten season. It encourages a commitment to fasting and prayer, aligning oneself with Christ's strength to endure suffering and resist the temptations of the world.

The story within this piece acknowledges the reality that, like Jesus, we may face challenges from sin, whether in the flesh or spirit. However, it declares a steadfast hope in Christ as the Victor in the wilderness, asking that those who follow Him may not faint or fail in the face of adversity.

The hymn concludes with a vision of the peace divine that comes from such dedication - a holier gladness, with angels shining around those who faithfully serve Christ. The final plea is a heartfelt prayer for Jesus to keep His followers constantly by His side, so that they may appear with Him at the eternal Eastertide, symbolising the ultimate victory over sin and the celebration of resurrection.

Narrative: The verses narrate the story of Jesus' journey into the wilderness, focusing on the challenges and temptations he faced during the 40 days of fasting. It's a contemplative hymn that invites us to reflect on the solemnity of the Lenten season.

Musical Tone: With its measured and contemplative tempo, the music creates a tone of introspection. It conveys the seriousness of the story through a mood of reflection and preparation.

Devotional

Dear God, as we begin this season of reflection and preparation, we thank you for the example of Jesus, who spent forty days in the wilderness. Help us navigate our own journey, seeking your guidance and strength each day of this Lenten season.

Matthew 4:1–11

"Then Jesus was led by the Spirit into the wilderness to be tempted by the devil. After fasting forty days and forty nights, he was hungry. The tempter came to him and said, 'If you are the Son of God, tell these stones to become bread.' Jesus answered, 'It is written: "Man shall not live on bread alone, but on every word that comes from the mouth of God."

In this passage, Jesus is led into the wilderness by the Holy Spirit, where he undergoes a period of fasting for forty days. Satan tempts him with the suggestion to turn stones into bread, but Jesus responds by affirming the greater importance of spiritual nourishment over physical sustenance.

Prayer

As I navigate the challenges of self-discipline during this Lenten season, may I remember that true sustenance comes from Your Word. Help me prioritise spiritual nourishment over worldly desires. In moments of temptation, may Your truth guide me.

Evening Devotional

As the day transitions into evening, I reflect on the humble shepherds, finding meaning in their response to the call of worship. In the quiet moments of this night, I acknowledge the message that echoes through the ages - the promise of salvation brought by the Messiah. May my heart be filled with adoration as I recognise the sacred in the ordinary. In this moment of reflection, I offer gratitude for the day's experiences and seek solace in the simplicity of the Nativity story that continues to inspire and guide us.

2
Lord, Who Throughout These Forty Days
Claudia Frances Hernaman

Lord, who throughout these forty days,
For us did fast and pray,
Teach us with you to mourn our sins,
And close by you to stay.

As you with Satan did contend,
And did the vict'ry win,
O give us strength in you to fight,
In you to conquer sin.

As you did hunger bear and thirst,
So teach us, gracious Lord,
To die to self, and always live
By your most holy word.

And through these days of penitence,
And through your Passion-tide,
Forevermore, in life and death,
O Lord, with us abide.

Abide with us that when this life
Of suffering is past,
An Easter of unending joy
We may attain at last!

Authorship

Claudia Frances Hernaman, born in 1838, emerged as a notable hymn writer whose contributions have enriched Christian worship over the years. Formerly Claudia Frances Ibotson, she later married Reverend Charles William Reynell Hernaman.

One of her enduring works is "Lord, Who Throughout These Forty Days," a hymn that resonates with congregations globally. Its verses eloquently convey the spiritual significance of the Lenten season, capturing the essence of faith with timeless messages.

Her hymns, distinguished by lyrical beauty and theological depth, reflect a devotion to Christian themes. Through her creative endeavours and writing she exemplifies the enduring impact individuals can have on the spiritual expression of communities. "Lord, Who Throughout These Forty Days" remains a lasting legacy in Christian hymnal worship.

The story within the hymn

"Lord, Who Throughout These Forty Days" is as a prayerful reflection on the season of Lent. The lyrics contemplate Christs journey, echoing the 40 days Jesus spent fasting in the wilderness. The hymn reads as a prayer for strength and guidance during the Lenten season. Its lyrics acknowledging the challenges faced during this period, and seeking God's help in navigating through it.

Each verse looks at a different aspect of the Lenten experience, encouraging us to seek strength, guidance, and spiritual transformation during this period of introspection. The story throughout addresses themes of repentance, self-discipline, and the overarching need for divine assistance in navigating our own personal challenges. It provides a structured and poetic means to collectively engage with the biblical narrative of Jesus' 40 days in the desert.

As we follow the hymn, we join in a communal plea for God's presence and grace to accompany us throughout Lent and beyond. Hernaman's evocative language and thoughtful composition make "Lord, Who Throughout These Forty Days" a timeless piece, connecting people across generations to the profound significance of this season.

Narrative: The verses tell the story of the Christian journey through the season of Lent, recognising the need for divine guidance and strength. It's a hymn that serves as a spiritual guide helping us seek God's presence and support during this season.

Musical Tone: With its gentle and supplicating melodies the music creates a tone of humility and dependence, whilst its harmonies convey a mood of earnest prayer, enhancing the narrative of seeking God's guidance.

Devotional

Lord, as we journey through these forty days, grant us the wisdom to reflect on our lives, the courage to face challenges, and the strength to grow spiritually. May this Lenten season be a time of transformation and renewal.

Joel 2:12-13

"Even now," declares the Lord, "return to me with all your heart, with fasting and weeping and mourning." Rend your heart and not your garments. Return to the Lord your God, for he is gracious and compassionate, slow to anger and abounding in love, and he relents from sending calamity."

This verse encourages us to turn back to God with our whole hearts, expressing genuine sorrow for our wrongdoings. It reminds us that God is compassionate and forgiving.

Prayer

Dear God, I turn to You with all my heart. I'm sorry for my mistakes. Please help me grow closer to You, knowing that You are loving and merciful.

3
Alas! And Did My Saviour Bleed?
Isaac Watts

Alas! and did my Saviour bleed,
And did my Sovereign die!
Would he devote that sacred head
For sinners such as I?

Was it for crimes that I have done,
He groaned upon the tree?
Amazing pity! Grace unknown!
And love beyond degree!

Well might the sun in darkness hide,
And shut its glories in,
When God, the mighty maker, died
For his own creature's sin.

Thus might I hide my blushing face
While his dear cross appears;
Dissolve my heart in thankfulness,
And melt mine eyes to tears.

But drops of tears can ne'er repay
The debt of love I owe.
Here, Lord, I give myself away;
'Tis all that I can do.

Authorship

Isaac Watts, often known as the "Father of English Hymnody," wrote "Alas! and Did My Saviour Bleed" in 1707. This hymn is a moving expression of gratitude for the sacrifice of Jesus on the cross. Born on July 17, 1674, in Southampton, England, he left an enduring legacy as a prominent Christian minister, hymn writer, theologian, and logician. Renowned for revolutionising congregational singing, Watts's hymns departed from the prevailing psalm-singing tradition by introducing original poetic compositions that conveyed profound theological insights in a more accessible and emotionally resonant manner.

His prolific hymn-writing career, which flourished in the late 17th and early 18th centuries, produced timeless classics such as "Joy to the World," "When I Survey the Wondrous Cross," and "O God, Our Help in Ages Past." Watts's hymns, marked by their eloquence and spiritual depth, continue to enrich worship services globally, attesting to his enduring influence on Christian hymnody. His contributions not only transformed the landscape of religious music but also solidified his place as a key figure in the history of Christian worship.

The story within the hymn

"Alas! and Did My Saviour Bleed", which is also known as "At the Cross", tells the heartfelt story of Christ's sacrificial love on the cross. The hymn takes us on a journey through the events of Good Friday, where each verse becomes a chapter in the emotional exploration of the crucifixion. The narrative begins with a lamentation, recognising the weight of Jesus' sacrifice and the painful cost of redemption.

As the hymn is sung, the words shifts from lament to gratitude in a moving response to the sacrificial act of love. The verses create a vivid portrayal of the the journey from darkness to light, from sin to salvation. The story explores the depths of divine mercy and prompts congregations to contemplate the immense price paid for their redemption. "Alas! and Did My Saviour Bleed" stands as a testament to the transformative power of the cross, inviting us to immerse ourselves in the profound narrative of love and redemption.

Narrative: The verses tell the story of the crucifixion, expressing astonishment and gratitude for the Saviour's willingness to bleed and die for the forgiveness of sins. It's a contemplative hymn that shows us the depth of Christ's sacrifice.

Musical Tone: The music, with its solemn and reverent tones, creates a sense of deep contemplation, conveying a mood of awe and reverence, and enhancing the emotional impact of the story within.

Devotional

Gracious Saviour, as we reflect on your sacrifice on the cross, we are humbled by the depth of your love. Help us to truly comprehend the cost of our redemption and respond with sincere gratitude and commitment to live in accordance with your teachings.

Matthew 4:11

"Then Jesus was led by the Spirit into the wilderness to be tempted by the devil. After fasting forty days and forty nights, he was hungry. The tempter came to him and said, 'If you are the Son of God, tell these stones to become bread.' Jesus answered, 'It is written: "Man shall not live on bread alone, but on every word that comes from the mouth of God."

In this passage, Jesus is led into the wilderness by the Holy Spirit, where he undergoes a period of fasting for forty days. The devil tempts him with the suggestion to turn stones into bread, but Jesus responds by affirming the greater importance of spiritual nourishment over physical sustenance. This shows us the importance of self-discipline and resisting temptations, teaching us that during times of struggle, we can find strength through faith.

Prayer

Lord, as I navigate the challenges of self-discipline during these forty days help me find strength in You and prioritise spiritual nourishment over worldly desires. In moments of temptation, may Your truth guide me

4
O Sacred Head, Now Wounded
Paul Gerhardt

O sacred Head, now wounded,
With grief and shame weighed down,
Now scornfully surrounded
With thorns, Thine only crown.
O sacred Head, what glory,
What bliss till now was Thine!
Yet, though despised and gory,
I joy to call Thee mine.

What Thou, my Lord, hast suffered
Was all for sinners' gain;
Mine, mine was the transgression,
But Thine the deadly pain.
Lo, here I fall, my Saviour!
'Tis I deserve Thy place;
Look on me with Thy favour,
Vouchsafe to me Thy grace.

What language shall I borrow
To thank Thee, dearest Friend,
For this, Thy dying sorrow,
Thy pity without end?
O make me Thine forever!
And should I fainting be,
Lord, let me never, never
Outlive my love for Thee.

Be near when I am dying,
O show Thy cross to me!
And, for my succour flying,
Come, Lord, to set me free:
These eyes, new faith receiving,
From Thee shall never move;
For he who dies believing
Dies safely in Thy love.

Authorship

Paul Gerhardt, a towering figure in the landscape of Christian hymnody, was born in 1607 and left an indelible mark through his contributions, particularly his translation of the hymn "O Sacred Head, Now Wounded," originally attributed to Bernard of Clairvaux. Gerhardt, a Lutheran pastor in 17th-century Germany, faced numerous challenges during a period marked by religious turmoil and the devastating Thirty Years' War. Amidst these trials, his hymns, including the translated masterpiece "O Sacred Head, Now Wounded," became works of solace and reflection.

Gerhardt's ability to convey the themes of Bernard of Clairvaux's original Latin hymn into eloquent and emotionally resonant verses showcased his poetic prowess. The hymn, with its reflection on Christ's sacrifice, gained widespread popularity and has endured across centuries. Gerhardt's life was one of dedication to pastoral care and hymn writing, emphasising themes of hope, comfort, and unwavering faith in the face of adversity.

His hymns, often expressing a deep personal piety, not only enriched the spiritual lives of those in his immediate congregation, but also transcended cultural and linguistic boundaries, resonating with people worldwide. "O Sacred Head, Now Wounded" shows Gerhardt's ability to connect theology with the human experience, and to his enduring legacy as a hymn writer during a tumultuous period in history.

The story within the hymn

"O Sacred Head, Now Wounded" captures the intense suffering of Christ on the cross. The hymn reflects on the events of Good Friday, transporting us to the foot of the cross. Each verse paints a vivid emotional picture of the pain and love displayed on Calvary. It asks us to contemplate the sanctity of Jesus' head, bowed with grief and shame, as thorns encircle His crown.

In its simplest form this hymn is a powerful reflection on the suffering of Christ on the cross. The lyrics focus on the wounded head of Jesus crowned with thorns, conveying deep emotion and gratitude for His sacrifice. However the narrative in "O Sacred Head, Now Wounded" is not a detached retelling, but an immersive experience where each line helps us to enter into the story of Christ's sacrifice.

Delving into the significance of Jesus' suffering, the narrative emphasises that what He endured was for the benefit of sinners. It highlights personal transgressions, recognising them as the cause of the pain Jesus bore. The verses then contemplate the inadequacy of language where expressing gratitude becomes a challenge. Instead it offers an acknowledgment and thanks for the immeasurable sorrow endured. The plea to be made forever His, and the resolve to never outlive love for the Saviour, underscore the depth of our devotion.

As the hymn concludes, the focus shifts to a prayer for the presence of the cross during His final moments. It encourages us to seek solace and freedom in the Lord's imminent arrival. The commitment to unwavering faith and love, even in the face of death, is expressed with confidence that those who die believing do so safely in His love.

Narrative: The lyrics narrate the story of Jesus' journey to the cross, vividly portraying the suffering and agony experienced. It's a hymn that invites us to meditate on the sacrificial love displayed on Calvary, telling the story of Christ's ultimate sacrifice.

Musical Tone: With its mournful and poignant melodies creating a tone of deep emotion, the musical dynamics convey a mood of solemn reflection of Christ's suffering on the Cross.

Devotional

Dear Jesus, as we contemplate the wounds on your sacred head, we acknowledge the immense suffering you endured for our sake. May your sacrifice inspire us to live lives of compassion and love, recognising the dignity of every person.

Psalm 51:10

"Create in me a pure heart, O God, and renew a steadfast spirit within me."

This verse expresses a desire for a pure heart and a steadfast spirit, acknowledging that God has the power to transform us from within.

Prayer

God, create in me a clean heart and renew a steadfast spirit within me. Help me to be more like You in my thoughts and actions

5
Lead Me To Calvary
Jennie Evelyn Hussey

King of my life I crown Thee now -
Thine shall the glory be;
Lest I forget Thy thorn-crowned brow,
Lead me to Calvary.

Lest I forget Gethsemane,
Lest I forget Thine agony,
Lest I forget Thy love for me,
Lead me to Calvary.

Show me the tomb where Thou wast laid,
Tenderly mourned and wept;
Angels in robes of light arrayed
Guarded Thee whilst Thou slept.

Lest I forget Gethsemane,
Lest I forget Thine agony,
Lest I forget Thy love for me,
Lead me to Calvary.

Let me like Mary, thru the gloom,
Come with a gift to Thee;
Show to me now the empty tomb -
Lead me to Calvary.

Lest I forget Gethsemane,
Lest I forget Thine agony,
Lest I forget Thy love for me,
Lead me to Calvary.

May I be willing, Lord, to bear
Daily my cross for Thee;
Even Thy cup of grief to share -
Thou hast borne all for me.

Lest I forget Gethsemane,
Lest I forget Thine agony,
Lest I forget Thy love for me,
Lead me to Calvary.

Authorship

Jennie Evelyn Hussey, born in 1874, was a notable hymn writer whose life and work left an enduring impact on Christian worship. Despite facing physical challenges due to a childhood illness affecting her vision, Hussey's unwavering faith and poetic talents shone through in her hymn "Lead Me to Calvary." Born in a Quaker family, she later became affiliated with the Methodist Church.

"Lead Me to Calvary," one of her most well-known compositions, reflects her deep contemplation on the crucifixion. The hymn's heartfelt verses invite worshippers to reflect on the journey to Calvary and consider the significance of Christ's redemptive act of sacrifice. Hussey's ability to convey complex theological themes with simplicity and emotional resonance is a hallmark of her style.

Her life, marked by her dedication to her faith despite physical limitations, serves as a poignant backdrop to her hymn-writing endeavours. Her lyrical contributions characterised by a sense of devotion and contemplation, have stood the test of time. "Lead Me to Calvary" remains a powerful expression of worship resonating with people around the world and enriching their spiritual lives.

The story within the hymn

"Lead Me to Calvary" is a deeply personal story of devotion and surrender. Each verse takes a step along the path to the cross, where expressing a heartfelt plea for divine guidance. The themes of redemption and forgiveness also invite us to reflect on the profound impact of Christ's sacrifice.

The lyrics express a personal longing to be led to the place where it took place, recognising it as the source of transformation. It becomes a journey of surrender, inviting us to lay our burdens and sins at the cross.

Narrative: The verses narrate the story of a personal plea for guidance to the foot of the cross, emphasising the power found in Christ's sacrifice. It's a hymn that tells the story of a soul yearning for redemption and forgiveness.

Musical Tone: With gentle and melancholy tones the music creates a mood of personal longing. The harmonies convey a mood of humility and earnest seeking, enhancing the desire of a soul's plea for guidance to Calvary.

Devotional

Loving Savior, lead us to the cross of Calvary each day and guide us in our journey of repentance and redemption. May we find forgiveness and renewal at the foot of the cross, experiencing the transformative power of your love.

Isaiah 58:6-7

"Is not this the kind of fasting I have chosen: to loose the chains of injustice and untie the cords of the yoke, to set the oppressed free and break every yoke? Is it not to share your food with the hungry and to provide the poor wanderer with shelter - when you see the naked, to clothe them, and not to turn away from your own flesh and blood?"

This passage underscores God's emphasis on acts of compassion and justice over religious rituals. It challenges us to redefine fasting, emphasising the importance of actively addressing social injustices and demonstrating compassion towards those in need. It calls for tangible, compassionate actions, encouraging us to actively participate in alleviating the suffering of others as a genuine expression of faith.

Prayer

Lord, show me how to live out my faith by helping those in need. May my actions reflect Your love and compassion for all people.

6

When I Survey The Wondrous Cross
Isaac Watts

When I survey the wondrous cross
On which the Prince of glory died,
My richest gain I count but loss,
And pour contempt on all my pride.

Forbid it, Lord, that I should boast
Save in the death of Christ, my God!
All the vain things that charm me most,
I sacrifice them through his blood.

See, from his head, his hands, his feet,
Sorrow and love flow mingled down.
Did e'er such love and sorrow meet,
Or thorns compose so rich a crown?

Were the whole realm of nature mine,
That were a present far too small.
Love so amazing, so divine,
Demands my soul, my life, my all.

Authorship

Another notable hymn by Isaac Watts (1674–1748), "When I Survey the Wondrous Cross" was published in 1707. A nonconformist minister and hymn writer, Watts who sought to bring emotional depth and personal reflection into congregational singing. See also Hymn 3, "Alas! Did My Saviour Bleed."

The story within the hymn

"When I Survey the Wondrous Cross" invites us to meditate on the meaning and significance of the cross through a narrative of contemplation and introspection. Each verse portrays the deep significance of the cross and the sacrifice it represents. It takes us into the heart of Christ's redemptive act, prompting us to survey, reflect, and respond to the overwhelming love displayed on the cross.

The hymns opening lines express a deep sense of humility, recognising that any worldly gain pales in comparison to the sacrifice on the cross, leading to a renouncement of personal pride. It then transitions to a plea to the Lord, emphasising the rejection of self-glorification and boasting, except in the death of Christ.

The sacrificial nature of Christ's death is highlighted as the hymn urges a willing surrender of worldly attractions through His redeeming blood. It portrays the physical suffering of Jesus on the cross, with sorrow and love depicted as mingling down from His head, hands, and feet. The imagery of thorns forming a rich crown evokes a sense of the cost of this love, asking if ever love and sorrow met in such an intense way.

Finally, the concluding lines express a surrender of all earthly possessions, to show that even if one possessed the entire realm of nature, it would be too small a gift in comparison to the divine love displayed on the cross. The hymn culminates in the acknowledgment that such love demands the totality of one's soul, life, and all. This hymn takes us to a place of deep introspection, where the story of the cross becomes a source of awe, gratitude, and spiritual renewal.

Narrative: The verses walk us through a personal reflection on the sacrifice of Jesus, acknowledging the unworthiness of the singer in the face of such divine love. The hymn culminates in a commitment to surrender everything in response to the cross.

Musical Tone: A slow and measured tempo enhances the contemplative mood and feeling. The gentle rise and fall of the melody mirrors the emotional weight of the lyrics, creating a somber and introspective tone.

Devotional

Lord, as we survey the wondrous cross, help us grasp the profound meaning of your sacrifice. May our hearts overflow with gratitude for your love, and may we respond by living lives that reflect the beauty of your redemption.

Luke 9:23

"Then he said to them all: 'Whoever wants to be my disciple must deny themselves and take up their cross daily and follow me'."

Jesus calls us to follow Him wholeheartedly, even if it means facing challenges. Taking up our cross daily symbolises a commitment to follow Christ, regardless of difficulties.

Prayer

Jesus, help me to follow You every day, even when it's hard. I commit to carrying my cross and following Your example of love and sacrifice.

7

The Strife is O'er, the Battle Done

Francis Pott (lyrics), Giovanni Palestrina (music),
William Henry Monk (arrangement)

The strife is o'er, the battle done;
The victory of life is won;
The song of triumph has begun.
Alleluia!

The powers of death have done their worst,
But Christ their legions has dispersed.
Let shouts of holy joy outburst.
Alleluia!
!

The three sad days are quickly sped;
He rises glorious from the dead.
All glory to our risen Head.
Alleluia!
He closed the yawning gates of hell;
The bars from heaven's high portals fell.
Let hymns of praise his triumph tell.
Alleluia!

Lord, by the stripes which wounded thee,
From death's dread sting thy servants free,
That we may live and sing to thee.
Alleluia!

Alleluia, alleluia, alleluia!

Authorship

"The Strife is O'er, the Battle Done" is a hymn that intertwines the contributions of Francis Pott who wrote the text, music by Giovanni Palestrina, and arrangement by William Henry Monk, reflecting the convergence of theological, social, and cultural influences across different periods in time.

Francis Pott (1832-1909), an Anglican clergyman and hymn writer, lived in a time marked by significant theological shifts and Victorian religious revival. The 19th century witnessed a resurgence of interest in hymnody as part of the Oxford Movement, an Anglican revival that sought a return to high church practices. Pott's hymn, with its triumphal Easter theme, resonates with the emphasis on Christ's victory over sin and death. As a clergyman, Pott's hymns often mirrored his own religious convictions, reflecting the evolving landscape of Victorian Christianity. Beyond his hymnody, Pott served as a dedicated churchman, contributing to the spiritual life of his community.

Giovanni Palestrina (1525-1594), a Renaissance composer, lived during a period of profound religious and cultural changes marked by the Council of Trent (1545-1563). During the Council of Trent the Catholic Church convened to address challenges posed by the Protestant Reformation. The Council played a role in shaping the religious and sacred music of the time aiming to reform and clarify various aspects of Catholic doctrine, liturgy, and music. Palestrina's life and works were situated in this context.

His compositions, including the original music for this hymn, reflect the Council's desire for clarity and reverence in church music. Palestrina is known for his ability to harmonise complex music with a sense of clarity, seeking a balance between the beauty of music and the intelligibility of the text. His influence extended beyond his lifetime, and his compositions remain significant in the history of Western sacred music.

William Henry Monk (1823-1889), an English organist and music editor, lived during the Victorian era. This period witnessed both social and industrial changes, with a growing interest in hymnody as part of the broader evangelical revival. Monk's arrangement of Palestrina's music for "The Strife is O'er, the Battle Done" reflects the Victorian enthusiasm for adapting and reviving earlier musical works. Monk was a notable figure in the 19th-century English church music scene, and his contributions extended beyond this arrangement to include the famous tune "Abide with Me." His work as an editor and composer had a lasting impact on hymnody, contributing to the rich musical heritage of Victorian Christianity.

"The Strife is O'er, the Battle Done" emerges as a hymn that weaves together the theological depth of Francis Pott, the Renaissance musical heritage of Giovanni Palestrina, and the Victorian musical sensibilities of William Henry Monk. This collaboration reflects not only their individual contributions, but also the broader currents of theological, social, and cultural influences that shaped Christian worship during their respective times.

The story within the hymn

"The Strife is O'er, the Battle Done" is a hymn that tells the story of the resurrection of Jesus Christ, celebrating the victory over death and the triumphant conclusion of the battle against sin and darkness.

The hymn opens with a proclamation that the struggle is over, and the battle has been won. It joyfully announces the triumph of Jesus over the forces of death and evil. The word "Alleluia" is a joyful expression of praise and celebration, emphasising the significance of this victorious moment. The lyrics vividly describe the impact of Jesus' victory, stating that death's mightiest powers have done their worst. The foes of Jesus have been dispersed, and the hymn encourages shouts of praise and joy. It paints a picture of the defeated enemies and the magnitude of Christ's triumph. The story then turns to the resurrection morning, highlighting the pivotal moment when Jesus rises from the dead. The lyrics joyfully declare that on the third day Jesus emerged glorious in majesty, signalling the end of the sorrowful period and the beginning of a new era of hope and life.

The hymns imagery proclaims Jesus as the one who closed the gates of hell and broke the bars from heaven's high portals. It conveys the idea that through His death and resurrection He conquered death and opened the way to eternal life. It emphasises the power and authority of Christ over the spiritual realms.

The hymn closes with a plea to the Lord, acknowledging His sacrificial death by the stripes that wounded Him. By embracing His triumph we can lead a life of praise and song. Overall, "The Strife is O'er, the Battle Done" is a hymn of celebration. It tells the story of Jesus' victorious resurrection, emphasising the defeat of death and the restoration of hope for believers. The hymn is a joyful proclamation of the central Christian message – that through the death and resurrection of Jesus, the battle against sin and death has been decisively won.

Narrative: Celebrating Jesus' triumph over death, this hymn exudes joy and hope, vividly expressing the decisive victory of Christ and inviting us to join in the celebration of redemption.

Musical tone: Musically, the hymn's triumphant and uplifting tone creates an atmosphere of joy and gratitude, perfectly complementing the exuberant narrative of Christ's resurrection.

Devotional

Dear God, thank you for Jesus' victory over challenges. Help me face each day with confidence and joy, remembering the hope found in His triumph. Amen.

2 Corinthians 7:10

"Godly sorrow brings repentance that leads to salvation and leaves no regret, but worldly sorrow brings death."

This verse emphasises the transformative power of true repentance. Genuine remorse leads to positive change and salvation, while regret only brings sorrow.

Prayer

God, help me to genuinely repent of my mistakes. May my sorrow lead to positive change, and may I find peace in Your forgiveness.

8
What Wondrous Love Is This
Anonymous

What wondrous love is this, O my soul, O my soul!
What wondrous love is this, O my soul!
What wondrous love is this, that caused the Lord of bliss
to bear the dreadful curse for my soul, for my soul,
to bear the dreadful curse for my soul.

When I was sinking down, sinking down, sinking down,
when I was sinking down, O my soul!
When I was sinking down beneath God's righteous frown,
Christ laid aside His crown for my soul, for my soul,
Christ laid aside His crown for my soul.

To God and to the Lamb I will sing, I will sing;
to God and to the Lamb, I will sing.
To God and to the Lamb who is the great "I AM,"
while millions join the theme, I will sing, I will sing,
while millions join the theme, I will sing.

Authorship

"What Wondrous Love Is This," an anonymous traditional American folk hymn, embodies the rich cultural and religious heritage of Christian devotion in 19th-century America. Emerging from the folk traditions of the time, the hymn reflects spirituality across diverse communities throughout the nation.

Rooted in the socio-religious fabric of early America, where communal singing and hymnody played a central role in worship, the hymn served as a poignant expression of the Christian experience.

The 19th century was marked by a fervent religious revival known as the Second Great Awakening, which swept across America, fostering a deepened sense of piety and spiritual introspection. The hymn's haunting melody and heartfelt lyrics resonated with the fervour of this era, capturing the collective yearning for a deeper connection with the divine.

Within the folk traditions of the time, the anonymity of hymn authors was not uncommon, highlighting the communal nature of worship and emphasising that the hymn was not the creation of a single individual but rather a shared expression of faith. "What Wondrous Love Is This" became a musical vessel through which believers could unite in their shared experiences of awe and gratitude for the redemptive love of God.

As a product of its cultural and religious time, the hymn captures the spirit of congregational singing that was integral to the worship practices of 19th-century America. Its continued resonance in diverse Christian denominations and presence in worship settings worldwide speak to the timeless power of this traditional American folk hymn.

The story within the hymn

"What Wondrous Love Is This" explores the depth and uniqueness of God's love, particularly as demonstrated through the sacrifice of Christ. Its lyrics are written to marvel at the extraordinary nature of God's love shown for our souls. The repeated question, "What wondrous love is this, O my soul?" underscores the awe and amazement at the depth of this divine love. The lyrical portrayal of the Lord of bliss willingly bearing a dreadful curse for our souls also depicts the sacrificial nature of this love.

The second verse recounts a personal experience of being in a low, sinking state, emphasising the idea of spiritual descent beneath God's righteous disapproval. In this moment, the hymn paints a vivid image of Christ, choosing to lay aside His crown, a symbol of majesty and authority, for the sake of our souls. This act of humility and sacrifice resonates as a powerful expression of love. The third verse shifts the focus to a commitment to praise both God and the Lamb, symbolising Jesus Christ. The reference to the Lamb as the great "I AM" echoes the divinity of Christ. The resolve to sing and join the theme with millions also reflects a collective acknowledgment of the boundless love that is being celebrated. The repetition of "I will sing" underscores the joyful commitment to express gratitude and adoration for this wondrous love. Collectively, "What Wondrous Love Is This" guides us through a contemplative journey, prompting reflection on the sacrificial love extended to our souls. It encourages a personal response of gratitude and a communal celebration of this extraordinary love.

Narrative: The verses tell a story of God's profound love expressed through the sacrifice of Jesus on the cross. It emphasises the inexplicable and wondrous nature of this love, inviting singers and listeners to reflect on its transformative power.

Musical Tone: Soulful and expressive melodies conveying a sense of awe and marvel, with rising and falling dynamics enhancing the emotional and reverent feeling.

Devotional

God of wondrous love, as we reflect on the depth of your love, fill our hearts with awe and gratitude. May your love transform us and empower us to love others with the same selfless devotion that you have shown us.

Isaiah 40:31

"Those who hope in the Lord will renew their strength. They will soar on wings like eagles; they will run and not grow weary, they will walk and not be faint."

This verse encourages us to trust in God during challenging times. Those who put their hope in God will find renewed strength and endurance.

Prayer

Lord, I place my hope in You. Renew my strength like eagles' wings, so I can face challenges with endurance and faith.

9

Ah, Holy Jesus, How Hast Thou Offended
Johann Heermann

Ah, holy Jesus, how hast thou offended,
That we to judge thee have in hate pretended?
By foes derided, by thine own rejected,
O most afflicted!

Who was the guilty? Who brought this upon thee?
Alas, my treason, Jesus, hath undone thee!
'Twas I, Lord Jesus, I it was denied thee;
I crucified thee.

Lo, the Good Shepherd for the sheep is offered;
The slave hath sinned, and the Son hath suffered.
For our atonement, while we nothing heeded,
God interceded.

For me, kind Jesus, was thy incarnation,
Thy mortal sorrow, and thy life's oblation;
Thy death of anguish and thy bitter passion,
For my salvation.

Therefore, kind Jesus, since I cannot pay thee,
I do adore thee, and will ever pray thee,
Think on thy pity and thy love unswerving,
Not my deserving.

Authorship

Johann Heermann, a German Lutheran pastor and hymn writer born in 1585, made a significant impact on Christian hymnody during the tumultuous period of the Thirty Years' War. One of his notable hymns is "Ah, Holy Jesus, How Hast Thou Offended," a reflection on the crucifixion and the human condition. Heermann's life unfolded against a backdrop of religious and political upheaval, and he personally experienced the devastating effects of the war.

Heermann's hymns, deeply influenced by his own experiences and the theological currents of his time, became sources of solace and theological reflection for those facing adversity. "Ah, Holy Jesus" stands out for its moving verses that invite worshippers to contemplate the suffering of Christ. Heermann's hymnody was characterised by a rich blend of theological depth and poetic beauty, and his contributions played a significant role in shaping Lutheran hymnody.

The English translation of "Ah, Holy Jesus" by Robert Bridges introduced this powerful hymn to a broader audience, further contributing to its enduring popularity. Bridges, an English poet born in 1844, was the Poet Laureate of the United Kingdom and had a keen appreciation for the beauty of Heermann's original German text.

Both Heermann and Bridges, separated by centuries and cultural contexts, left lasting legacies through their collaborative effort on "Ah, Holy Jesus." Heermann's hymn continues to resonate with worshippers, offering an enduring meditation on the crucifixion, while Bridges' translation facilitated its reach to English-speaking congregations, ensuring its place in Christian hymnody.

The story within the hymn

In the reflective hymn "Ah, Holy Jesus," each verse encourages us to think about how much Jesus sacrificed for us, and our part in His suffering. The hymn starts with a powerful question, marveling at how Jesus, who is holy, was wrongly judged and hated. The imagery of Him being derided and rejected, depicted as "O most afflicted," sets a somber tone. The second verse delves into self-reflection on our own actions, asking who is to blame for Jesus' suffering. The answer points to our own responsibility. The words "I, Lord Jesus, I denied you; I crucified you," helps us to create a direct connection between our actions and Christ's crucifixion, fostering our sense of remorse and repentance.

The hymn then looks at Jesus as the Good Shepherd who gives Himself for His followers, recognising that we have sinned, and He suffered to save us. The idea that God steps in to make amends, even when we are indifferent, shows us a picture of divine mercy and grace. The fourth verse thinks about Jesus coming to earth, mortal sorrow and giving His life for our sake. The hymn expresses gratitude and thanks for these selfless acts and recognises how important they are for redemption.

The final verse acknowledges the inability to repay Jesus for such sacrificial love. Instead, it suggests showing love and continuous prayer asking for Jesus's compassion highlighting that we rely on grace, not our own goodness. Overall, "Ah, Holy Jesus" guides us through a journey of reflection, repentance, and gratitude, prompting contemplation for Jesus' sacrifice and the mercy He offers us.

Narrative: The verses are filled with contrition, recognising the offence committed against the Holy One. It's a profound reflection on the cost of redemption, and a call to seek mercy and forgiveness.

Musical Tone: With its somber and contemplative tones the music mirrors the penitential mood, with a minor key and restrained dynamics evoking a sense of humility and sorrow.

Devotional

Merciful Saviour, as we lament your suffering grant us a heart of contrition. Help us recognise the ways we fall short and seek your mercy. May our repentance be genuine, and may we strive to live in a manner that honours your sacrifice.

Philippians 3:10-11

"I want to know Christ - yes, to know the power of his resurrection and participation in his sufferings, becoming like him in his death, and so, somehow, attaining to the resurrection from the dead."

Paul expresses a deep desire to know Christ more intimately, sharing in His sufferings and resurrection. This verse encourages us to seek a profound connection with Christ.

Prayer

Jesus, I want to know You more intimately. Help me understand the power of Your resurrection and find strength in sharing both joy and challenges with You.

10
Go To Dark Gethsemane
James Montgomery

Go to dark Gethsemane,
You who feel the tempter's pow'r;
Your Redeemer's conflict see;
Watch with Him one bitter hour;
Turn not from His griefs away;
Learn of Jesus Christ to pray.

Follow to the judgment hall;
View the Lord of life arraigned;
O the worm-wood and the gall!
O the pangs His soul sustained!
Shun not suff'ring, shame, or loss;
Learn of Him to bear the cross.

Calv'ry's mournful mountain climb
There' adoring at His feet,
Mark the miracle of time,
God's own sacrifice complete:
"It is finished!" Hear the cry;
Learn of Jesus Christ to die.

> Early hasten to the tomb
> Where they laid his breathless clay;
> All is solitude and gloom;
> Who hath taken Him away?
> Christ is ris'n! He meets our eyes:
> Saviour, teach us so to rise.

Authorship

James Montgomery, a prominent English hymn writer and poet born in 1771, crafted his legacy during a period marked by societal and cultural transformations. Living in the late 18th and early 19th centuries, Montgomery witnessed the dynamic shifts of the Industrial Revolution and the fervour of social reform movements. Born in Scotland, he later settled in Sheffield, England, where he became known for his activism, journalism, and literary contributions.

Montgomery's hymn "Go to Dark Gethsemane" reflects the ethos of his time, blending poetry with theology. The hymn invites us to meditate on the scene of Christ's agony in the Garden of Gethsemane, drawing our attention to the emotional weight of Jesus' sacrifice. In an era marked by industrialisation and social upheaval, Montgomery's hymn provided a contemplative space within the context of changing societal landscapes.

As the editor of the Sheffield Iris newspaper, Montgomery used his platform to advocate for social justice, religious freedom, and humanitarian causes. This commitment to social issues is echoed in his hymns, which often carry themes of compassion and empathy. "Go to Dark Gethsemane" stands as a musical expression of both the Christian narrative and Montgomery's concerns.

The hymn's enduring appeal lies not only in its lyrical beauty, but also in its ability to resonate with the complexities of the human experience amid cultural shifts. Montgomery's life and works exemplify the intertwining of faith, art, and social consciousness during a pivotal time in history, making "Go to Dark Gethsemane" a thoughtful reflection of both the Christian story and the broader cultural currents of its time.

The story within the hymn

"Go to Dark Gethsemane" guides us to the solemn events in the Garden of Gethsemane, as we enter into the emotional struggle and anticipation of the crucifixion. The hymn is a journey through crucial moments of Christ's passion, encouraging deep contemplation and emulation. Reflecting on the pivotal moments before the crucifixion, is prompts us to consider the significance of this place as we accompany Jesus in the darkness to witness the depth of His surrender and the weight of His impending sacrifice.

The initial verse directs us to Gethsemane to witness our Redeemer's internal struggle. The call to watch with Him for one bitter hour emphasises the importance of not turning away from Christ's sorrows, but rather learning the profound act of prayer from Jesus Christ.

The hymn then transports us to the judgment hall, compelling us to observe Jesus standing trial. The vivid imagery of "wormwood and gall" underscores the intensity of the pangs Christ's soul endured during this tumultuous time. Here, wormwood symbolises bitterness and gall represents something profoundly unpleasant, adding depth to the description of His suffering. This encourages us not to shy away from suffering, shame, or loss but to learn from Christ how to bear the burdens of life.

Moving to Calvary's mournful mountain, the hymn then invites us to adore at Christ's feet, recognising the miraculous moment of God's own sacrifice. The declaration "It is finished!" resounds, urging us to learn from Jesus Christ the lesson of surrendering and letting go of our own desires.

The hymn's final verse prompts us to hasten to the tomb, where solitude and gloom reign after the crucifixion. The question arises: "Who hath taken Him away?" The revelation of the resurrection, with the exclamation "Christ is ris'n! He meets our eyes," instils hope and prompts a prayer for the Saviour to teach us to rise.

Collectively, "Go to Dark Gethsemane" guides us through the poignant moments of Christ's passion, imparting valuable lessons on prayer, endurance in the face of suffering, the sacrificial nature of His death, and transformative hope found in His resurrection.

Narrative: The verses tell the story of Jesus' agonising prayer in Gethsemane, grappling with his impending sacrifice. It's a heartfelt reflection on Christ's obedience and the weight of the forthcoming crucifixion.

Musical Tone: The music, with its haunting and contemplative melodies, sets a tone of solemn anticipation whilst gradual crescendos and decrescendos intensify the emotional depth of the story.

Devotional

Lord, as we face darkness we seek your strength in times of trial. Help us trust in your plan even when we face challenges and may the shadows of Gethsemane remind us of the light that awaits in your resurrection.

Psalm 103:8-14

> *"The Lord is compassionate and gracious, slow to anger, abounding in love. He will not always accuse, nor will he harbour his anger forever; he does not treat us as our sins deserve or repay us according to our iniquities. For as high as the heavens are above the earth, so great is his love for those who fear him; as far as the east is from the west, so far has he removed our transgressions from us. As a father has compassion on his children, so the Lord has compassion on those who fear him; for he knows how we are formed, he remembers that we are dust."*

This passage emphasises God's compassion, forgiveness, and understanding of our human frailty, reassuring us of God's love and willingness to forgive.

Prayer

Gracious God, thank You for Your compassion and forgiveness. Help me to extend the same love and understanding to others as You do to me.

Easter

As Lent draws to a close, paving the way for the Easter celebration, we shift our focus from the reflective journey of self-discipline through Lent to the joyous commemoration of Christ's resurrection. Easter, the pinnacle of Christian faith, marks the triumphant fulfilment of the promises made during the Lenten season.

Easter Sunday, the climax of this spiritual pilgrimage, beckons us to embrace the profound truth of Jesus overcoming death. It's a day of jubilation where shadows give way to the light of resurrection. As we gather let our hearts resonate with the triumphant declaration: He is risen!

The journey of Lent, with its emphasis on prayer, fasting, and almsgiving, prepares us for the transformative power encapsulated in Easter. The ashes of Ash Wednesday, a tangible symbol of repentance, now find their counterpoint in the empty tomb - a symbol of new life and redemption. The discipline practiced during Lent becomes the fertile ground for the seeds of joy to blossom on Easter Sunday.

Just as Lent serves as a mirror for self-examination, Easter is a proclamation of God's unyielding love. It's a reminder that, no matter how deep our reflections have been, the resurrection ushers in a season of hope. The Lenten sacrifices find their purpose in the celebration of Easter - not only as a historical event but of a living and present Saviour.

May this Easter be a source of enduring inspiration to you. Let it be a reminder that, just as Christ emerged from the tomb, we too can arise from the challenges and struggles of life.

As we celebrate the risen Lord, may our lives reflect the transformative power of Easter that brings redemption, renewal, and unending joy.

11
Christ the Lord is Risen Today
Charles Wesley

Christ the Lord is risen today, Alleluia!
Earth and heaven in chorus say, Alleluia!
Raise your joys and triumphs high, Alleluia!
Sing, ye heavens, and earth reply, Alleluia!

Love's redeeming work is done, Alleluia!
Fought the fight, the battle won, Alleluia!
Death in vain forbids him rise, Alleluia!
Christ has opened paradise, Alleluia!

Lives again our glorious King, Alleluia!
Where, O death, is now thy sting? Alleluia!
Once he died our souls to save, Alleluia!
Where's thy victory, boasting grave? Alleluia!

Soar we now where Christ has led, Alleluia!
Following our exalted Head, Alleluia!
Made like him, like him we rise, Alleluia!
Ours the cross, the grave, the skies, Alleluia!

Hail the Lord of earth and heaven, Alleluia!
Praise to thee by both be given, Alleluia!
Thee we greet triumphant now, Alleluia!
Hail the Resurrection, thou, Alleluia!

King of glory, soul of bliss, Alleluia!
Everlasting life is this, Alleluia!
Thee to know, thy power to prove, Alleluia!
Thus to sing, and thus to love, Alleluia!

Authorship

Charles Wesley, born in 1707, was not only a prolific hymn writer but also a co-founder of the Methodist movement alongside his brother, John Wesley. Raised in a devout Anglican family, Charles underwent a profound spiritual experience in 1738, leading to his active involvement in the Evangelical revival within the Church of England.

His hymns, including "Christ the Lord Is Risen Today," played a pivotal role in conveying the theological tenets of Methodism to a broader audience. In addition to his hymnody, Charles was a gifted preacher and an influential figure in the development of Methodist theology and liturgy. The hymn reflects not only the joyous celebration of Easter but also Charles Wesley's commitment to expressing Christian doctrine through the medium of congregational singing.

The story within the hymn

"Christ the Lord Is Risen Today" celebrates the resurrection of Jesus on Easter Sunday. In the opening lines, the hymn bursts forth with the triumphant announcement that Christ, the Lord, has risen today. This proclamation serves as the anthem of Easter, heralding the cornerstone of Christian faith – the resurrection of Jesus. The use of the word "risen" encapsulates the transformative event that defines Christianity, emphasising the victorious emergence from the grasp of death.

As we move into the lyrics that beckon the congregation to "raise your joys and triumphs high," Wesley invites worshippers into a communal celebration. The call to elevate both joys and triumphs reinforces the collective nature of the Easter proclamation. It's a shared exultation, an invitation for all believers to lift their spirits in recognition of the profound victory of Christ over the grave.

"Alleluia!" punctuates the hymn, echoing through the verses as a recurring expression of praise. This term, deeply ingrained in religious language, creates a resounding chorus of joy and exultation. It serves as a collective utterance of gratitude and reverence, woven into the fabric of the hymn to amplify the jubilant atmosphere.

Moving through the verses that depict scenes of heavenly realms joining the celebration, the hymn broadens its scope painting a vivid picture of angelic choirs and triumphant hosts proclaiming the resurrection. This imagery creates a sense of cosmic rejoicing, portraying the magnitude of the event transcending earthly dimensions.

As the hymn progresses, the focus shifts to the temporal and eternal implications of Christ's resurrection. The lyric "Death in vain forbids His rise" encapsulates the futility of death's attempt to thwart the triumph of life. It underscores the decisive victory of Jesus over mortality and opens a gateway to eternal hope for believers.

In the final verse, Wesley's lyrics brings together the essence of Easter joy. They become a timeless proclamation, inviting everyone across generations to join the chorus of praise. It's an acknowledgment of the enduring significance of the resurrection, resonating through time as a source of hope, joy, and salvation.

In essence, "Christ the Lord Is Risen Today" is a vibrant celebration of praise and proclamation. Charles Wesley crafted a hymn that not only captures the theological depth of the resurrection but also invites us to participate in a n expression of joy, gratitude, and eternal hope together.

Narrative: The verses tell the story of Christ's triumph over the grave, expressing the exultant joy of Easter. It's a proclamation of victory and an invitation to join in the celebration of the risen Lord.

Musical Tone: The music, with its lively tunes, creates a tone of celebration with its spirited dynamics and harmonies mirroring the uplifting story of Easter triumph.

Devotional

Joyful Christ, on this Easter Sunday, we celebrate your resurrection with hearts full of love and hope. May the victory of your rising inspire us to live each day with the assurance that, in you, we find new life and eternal triumph.

Matthew 28:6

"He is not here; he has risen, just as he said. Come and see the place where he lay."

This verse announces the joyous news of Jesus' resurrection, emphasising that He is alive by inviting people to see the empty tomb where he lay.

Prayer

Lord Jesus, thank You for conquering death. I celebrate Your resurrection and find hope in the promise of eternal life with You.

12

He Is Risen, He Is Risen!

Cecil Frances Alexander

He is risen! He is risen!
Tell it out with joyful voice:
He has burst the three days' prison,
Let the whole wide earth rejoice:
Death is conquered, we are free,
Christ has won the victory.

He is risen! He is risen!
Christ has won the victory.

Come, ye sad and fearful-hearted,
With glad smile as brightest sun:
Night's long shadows have departed;
All His suff'ring now is done,
And the passion that He bore;
Sin and pain can harm no more.

He is risen! He is risen!
Christ has won the victory.

He is risen! He is risen!
Risen to a holy state:
We are free from sin's dark prison,
He has opened heaven's gate.

Death is conquered, we are free;
Christ has won the victory.

He is risen! He is risen!
Christ has won the victory.

Authorship

Cecil Frances Alexander, born in 1818 in County Tyrone, Ireland, was a prominent hymn writer and poet in the Anglican tradition. The wife of William Alexander, the Anglican Archbishop of Armagh, Cecil Frances Alexander wrote hymns that reflected her deep Christian faith and a desire to convey biblical truths in a poetic and accessible manner. Living in the midst of social and political challenges in 19th-century Ireland, Alexander dedicated herself to philanthropy and established a school for the deaf, emphasising her commitment to social welfare.

"He Is Risen, He Is Risen!" is one of her numerous hymns that catered to the spiritual needs of both children and adults, showcasing her dedication to Christian education. Her hymns, characterised by simplicity and religious insights, became enduring contributions to the hymnody of the Anglican Church and beyond.

The story within the hymn

This popular Easter hymn begins with a resounding declaration that "He is risen!" The repetition through each verse emphasising the magnitude of the event being proclaimed – the resurrection of Jesus Christ. The exclamation mark also serves as a punctuation of triumph, setting the tone for a hymn that celebrates this core tenet of Christianity.

As we progress the verses describe the tomb where Jesus lay. The imagery of the sealed stone and watchful soldiers creates a sense of suspense. The hymn sets the stage for the triumphant impact of the resurrection. The lyrics unfold with the dramatic revelation that "He is risen!" This exuberant refrain reaffirms serves as a jubilant response to the anticipation built in the preceding lines becoming a rallying cry of victory over death.

Alexander then depicts a profound encounter as Mary Magdalene finds the living Jesus in the garden, adding a personal dimension to the resurrection story. It becomes a moment of realisation and transformation, marking the transition from despair to overwhelming joy.

As we approach the concluding verses, the words expand their focus to the broader implications of the resurrection. The assurance that "He is risen" becomes a source of comfort and hope, taking us beyond the historical event to resonate as a timeless truth.

In the final verse, Alexander's lyrics express the universal impact of Christ's resurrection as imagery of spring and renewal metaphorically aligns with the spiritual renewal brought about by the risen Saviour. It is an anthem of assurance of the transformative and life-giving power of the resurrection.

In essence, "He Is Risen, He Is Risen!" is a dynamic and vivid story of the resurrection. It artfully combines detailed imagery, personal encounters, and universal truths, creating a hymn that not only recounts the historical event but also invites us to experience the enduring impact of the risen Christ in our lives.

Narrative: Telling the triumphant story of the empty tomb and the realisation that Jesus has risen, the narrative of this hymn celebrates this momentous event and the hope it brings to humanity.

Musical Tone: The music, with its energetic and uplifting tone, creates a tone of celebration, whilst rises and falls in the melody reflect the emotional highs and lows of the moment of the resurrection.

Devotional

Triumphant Saviour, we announce and celebrate your resurrection with joyous hearts. As we bask in the light of your victory over death, may we be filled with the certainty that, because you live, we too can live abundantly and eternally.

1 Corinthians 15:20

"But Christ has indeed been raised from the dead, the first fruits of those who have fallen asleep."

Paul declares the significance of Christ's resurrection, assuring believers of the hope that comes through His victory over death.

Prayer

Jesus, as You are reborn, I trust in the promise of new life and hope that You bring to me.

13
Up from the Grave He Arose
Robert Lowry

Low in the grave He lay
Jesus my Saviour!
Waiting the coming day
Jesus my Lord!
Up from the grave He arose
With a mighty triumph o'er His foes
He arose a Victor from the dark domain
And He lives forever with His saints to reign
He arose! (He arose)
He arose! (He arose)
Hallelujah! Christ arose!

Vainly they watch His bed
Jesus, my Saviour!
Vainly they seal the dead
Jesus my Lord!
Up from the grave He arose
With a mighty triumph o'er His foes
He arose a Victor from the dark domain
And He lives forever with His saints to reign
He arose! (He arose)
He arose! (He arose)
Hallelujah! Christ arose!

Death cannot keep his prey
Jesus, my Saviour!
He tore the bars away
Jesus my Lord!
Up from the grave He arose
With a mighty triumph o'er His foes
He arose a Victor from the dark domain
And He lives forever with His saints to reign
He arose! (He arose)
He arose! (He arose)
Hallelujah! Christ arose!

Up from the grave He arose
With a mighty triumph o'er His foes
He arose a Victor from the dark domain
And He lives forever with His saints to reign
He arose! (He arose)
He arose! (He arose)
Hallelujah! Christ arose!

Authorship

Robert Lowry, born in 1826 in Philadelphia, Pennsylvania, was a Baptist minister, composer, and hymn writer who significantly influenced American hymnody in the 19th century. As a pastor, Lowry served churches in New York and New Jersey, contributing to the spiritual life of his congregations. Living in post-Civil War America, he witnessed the changes and challenges of Reconstruction across society. Lowry's hymns, characterised by their simplicity and emotional appeal, often addressed the hope and assurance found in Christian faith.

"Up from the Grave He Arose" is a prime example of Lowry's ability to convey the triumphant message of Christ's resurrection in a way that resonated with congregations facing the complexities of a nation in transition. Beyond his hymnody, Lowry was involved in music education and authored several books on hymnology, leaving a lasting impact on American Christian worship.

The story within the hymn

Up from the Grave He Arose" has a lively narrative vividly portraying the moment when Christ rises from the dead, conquering the grave and providing hope to all. It begins with a proclamation of the resurrection, setting the stage for a joyful reflection on this event. As the verses unfold, they paint a vivid picture of the empty tomb and the glorious moment of Christ's rising. The story invites us to join in the celebration, emphasising the tangible hope and assurance that the resurrection brings.

Narrative: The story throughout is a musical journey of exultation, prompting us to celebrate the transformative power of the resurrection. It brings us together in a celebration of joy, expressing gratitude for the risen Saviour who conquers death and brings new life, representing the eternal hope and triumphant meaning of Easter.

Musical Tone: Characterised by a lively tune, this piece has a tone of exultant rejoicing. It's energetic tempo and uplifting harmonies convey the joyous feeling surrounding the resurrection, setting a mood of celebratory triumph.

Devotional

Risen Lord, we rejoice in your triumph over the grave. Like a flower breaking through the soil, you emerged from death. May this Easter season be a reminder that, in you, we find resurrection and new beginnings.

John 11:25-26

"Jesus said to her, 'I am the resurrection and the life. The one who believes in me will live, even though they die'."

In this passage Jesus proclaims Himself as the resurrection and the life, offering eternal hope to those who believe in Him.

Prayer

Jesus, You are the source of life. Thank You for the promise of resurrection and eternal life. Help me live in the hope You provide.

14

Thine Be the Glory

Edmond Louis Budry, Richard Birch Hoyle (translation)

Thine be the glory, risen, conqu'ring Son;
Endless is the vict'ry Thou o'er death hast won.
Angels in bright raiment rolled the stone away,
Kept the folded grave-clothes where Thy body lay.

Thine be the glory, risen, conqu'ring Son;
endless is the vict'ry Thou o'er death hast won.

Lo! Jesus meets us, risen from the tomb.
Lovingly He greets us, scatters fear and gloom;
Let His church with gladness hymns of triumph sing,
For the Lord now liveth; death hath lost its sting.

Thine be the glory, risen, conqu'ring Son;
endless is the vict'ry Thou o'er death hast won.

No more we doubt Thee, glorious Prince of life!!
Life is nought without Thee; aid us in our strife;
Make us more than conqu'rors, through Thy deathless love;
Bring us safe through Jordan to Thy home above.

Thine be the glory, risen, conqu'ring Son;
endless is the vict'ry Thou o'er death hast won.

Authorship

"Thine Be the Glory," was originally written in French as "À toi la gloire" by Swiss pastor and hymn writer Edmond Louis Budry in the late 19th century. Born in 1854 in Vevey, Switzerland, Budry lived during a time of significant social and religious changes. The country, in the late 19th century, was undergoing a shift in cultural and religious landscapes, and Budry's hymn reflects the theological currents of this era.

As a pastor of the Free Evangelical Church in Vevey, Budry's hymn writing was influenced by his ministry, and the desire to provide his congregation with meaningful expressions of worship. "Thine Be the Glory" originally celebrated the resurrection of Christ, capturing the joy and victory inherent in the Easter message.

"Thine Be the Glory" was later translated into English by Richard Birch Hoyle, a British Congregational minister. Born in 1875, Hoyle contributed significantly to the English-speaking Christian community as a hymn translator and editor. Living in the early 20th century, he was witness to the aftermath of World War I, and his translation of "Thine Be the Glory" into English in the post-war years reflected a desire for hope and renewal in the face of global challenges. The hymn became particularly associated with Easter celebrations, embodying the triumph of life over death. This popular hymn demonstrates the enduring nature of Budry's original composition and Hoyle's translation skills and their collective contribution to Christian worship during a period marked by both local and global changes.

The story within the hymn

"Thine Be the Glory" is a well known and popular hymn with a celebratory narrative that honours the victory and glory of Christ over death and the grave. It's familiar and uplifting melodious proclamation of triumph creates a joyous declaration of the risen Lord. The story takes us on a journey of exuberance, prompting singers to join in a collective expression of praise for the victorious Christ. As it is sung worshipers are invited to enter into a narrative of gratitude and adoration, celebrating the resurrection as the ultimate manifestation of divine power. The hymn is a resounding memory to the glory that belongs to the risen Saviour and the eternal hope found in His triumph.

Narrative: The verses tell the story of the risen Christ, praising God for the triumph and declaring the impact of the resurrection on believers. It's a hymn of adoration and acknowledgment of divine glory.

Musical Tone: The music, with its majestic and triumphant melodies creates a tone of worship and praise. The powerful harmonies also amplify the celebratory mood, capturing the glory and enormity of the resurrection.

Devotional

Majestic God, we offer our praise and adoration to you, for the glory of your resurrection. May our lives reflect the splendour of your triumph, and may our worship be a testament to your eternal reign.

1 Peter 1:3

"Praise be to the God and Father of our Lord Jesus Christ! In his great mercy he has given us new birth into a living hope through the resurrection of Jesus Christ from the dead."

Peter praises God for the living hope we have through the resurrection of Jesus Christ from the dead.

Prayer

Heavenly Father, I'm grateful for the living hope I have in Christ. May Your resurrection power fill me with joy and confidence in Your promises."

15
Jesus Christ is Risen Today
Anonymous

Jesus Christ is ris'n today, alleluia!
Our triumphant holy day, alleluia!
Who did once, upon the cross, alleluia!
Suffer to redeem our loss, alleluia!

Hymns of praise then let us sing, alleluia!
Unto Christ, our heav'nly King, alleluia!
who endured the cross and grave, alleluia!
Sinners to redeem and save, alleluia!

But the pains which He endured, alleluia!
Our salvation have procured; alleluia!
Now above the sky He's King, alleluia!
Where the angels ever sing: alleluia!

Authorship

"Jesus Christ Is Risen Today" is an Easter hymn that has its roots in the 14th-century Bohemian Brethren hymn "Surrexit Christus hodie." The English language version we know today is attributed to an anonymous author and has undergone various adaptations over the centuries.

The hymn gained prominence in the 18th century when it was included in hymnals like "Lyra Davidica" (1708), a collection of hymns that aimed to revive and enrich congregational singing. The version we commonly sing today, with the "Allelujah" refrain, appeared in a later edition of "Lyra Davidica" in 1708.

During the 18th century, England experienced a hymn-singing revival, partly influenced by the work of writers like Isaac Watts. The societal context of the time saw a growing interest in congregational participation in worship, leading to the widespread adoption of hymns. "Jesus Christ Is Risen Today" became emblematic of this movement, embodying the joyful celebration of Christ's resurrection and providing a vibrant expression of Easter worship.

As the hymn traversed through various editions and adaptations, it continued to be embraced by different denominations and Christian communities, becoming a staple in Easter celebrations. Its enduring popularity speaks to its ability to capture the essence of the Easter message and to inspire people across generations.

The hymn's journey from medieval Bohemia to the 18th-century English hymn-singing revival reflects the diverse influences and cultural shifts that have shaped Christian hymnody over the centuries.

The story within the hymn

This ancient festive narrative rejoices in the resurrection of Jesus. Each verse is a joyful proclamation declaring Christ's victory over death. The story becomes a musical celebration of resurrection morning, prompting us to join in a collective expression of thanks and praise for the risen Saviour.

As it is sung, we enter into a narrative of joy, celebrating the transformative power of Easter and the eternal hope found in the resurrection. This short powerful hymn stands as a spirited testament to the triumphant narrative of resurrection day and the everlasting victory achieved through the risen Christ.

Narrative: The verses tell the story of the resurrection, inviting us to join in the celebration of Jesus' triumph. It's a jubilant proclamation of this central event in Christianity and its transformative impact on us all.

Musical Tone: With festive and lively tunes the music offers a tone of joyful celebration. Uplifting harmonies also create a mood of exuberance to resonate with the joyous narrative of Easter triumph.

Devotional

Resurrected Jesus, as we celebrate your resurrection today, may our hearts be filled with joy and our lives be a song of praise. May the reality of your victory shape our daily living and inspire us to share the good news with the world.

Luke 24:5-6

"In their fright the women bowed down with their faces to the ground, but the men said to them, 'Why do you look for the living among the dead? He is not here; he has risen!'"

This verse tells of the moment Angels announce Jesus' resurrection to the women, bringing a message of hope and assurance.

Prayer

Lord, Your resurrection brings joy and assurance, help me to live each day in the light of Your victorious love.

16

The Day of Resurrection

John Mason Neale

The day of resurrection!
Earth, tell it out abroad;
The passover of gladness,
The passover of God.
From death to life eternal,
From earth unto the sky,
Our Christ hath brought us over,
With hymns of victory.

Our hearts be pure from evil,
That we may see aright
The Lord in rays eternal
Of resurrection light;
And listening to his accents,
May hear, so calm and plain,
His own "All hail!" and, hearing,
May raise the victor strain.

Now let the heavens be joyful!
Let earth the song begin!
Let the round world keep triumph,
And all that is therein!
Let all things seen and unseen
Their notes in gladness blend,

> For Christ the Lord hath risen,
> Our joy that hath no end.

Authorship

"The Day of Resurrection," a hymn with roots in the Eastern Orthodox liturgy, was translated into English by John Mason Neale, a 19th-century Anglican clergyman and hymn writer. Born in London in 1818, Neale was a scholar with a deep interest in liturgies, hymnody, and ecclesiastical history. Living during the Victorian era, he witnessed a period marked by a revival of interest in medieval and Eastern Christian traditions.

Neale's life was characterised by a commitment to religious and historical scholarship. He faced opposition within the Anglican Church for his Tractarian views, which emphasised a return to pre-Reformation liturgical practices. Despite challenges, Neale co-founded the Society of Saint Margaret, an Anglican religious community for women, and devoted himself to the study and translation of hymns from various Christian traditions.

"The Day of Resurrection" reflects Neale's passion for making the rich heritage of Eastern Christian hymnody accessible to English-speaking congregations. His translations, including this hymn, played a crucial role in introducing the Western Christian world to the beauty and depth of Eastern liturgical texts. Through his scholarly pursuits and hymn writing, John Mason Neale left an enduring impact on Victorian-era Anglicanism, contributing to a broader appreciation for the diversity of Christian worship traditions.

The story within the hymn

"The Day of Resurrection" unfolds as an exuberant story, capturing the joyous essence of the resurrection. Each verse invites us to enter into the celebratory atmosphere of resurrection day, allowing congregations to join in a collective expression of exultation and praise for the risen Saviour. The verses are a celebration of victory over death, prompting us to rejoice in the transformative power of Easter. Singers and listeners enter into a narrative of jubilation, celebrating the resurrection as the dawn of eternal hope and new life. The hymn remains a joyous narrative of resurrection day and the everlasting victory achieved through the risen Christ.

Narrative: The verses of this hymn tell the story of the resurrection, emphasising the joyous reality of Christ conquering the grave. It's a hymn that invites us to join in the celebration of Easter through the dawn of new life and the eternal victory.

Musical Tone: The music, characterised by vibrant and triumphant melodies, creates a tone of praise and celebration setting a mood of jubilation of the Easter triumph as Christ is reborn.

Devotional

God of Resurrection, on this day of celebration, we express our gratitude for the promise of new life found in Christ. May this day mark the beginning of renewed hope and a deeper understanding of your transformative power in our lives.

Colossians 3:1-2

"Since, then, you have been raised with Christ, set your hearts on things above, where Christ is, seated at the right hand of God."

Paul encourages believers, having experienced the resurrection with Christ, to redirect their attention towards heavenly matters where Christ is seated at God's right hand. This advice underscores the importance of maintaining a spiritual perspective and prioritiSing meaningful aspects of life.

Prayer

Lord Jesus, help me focus on the eternal, knowing that You are alive and reigning. May my thoughts and actions reflect Your resurrection power.

17
I Know That My Redeemer Lives
Samuel Medley

I know that my Redeemer lives;
What comfort this sweet sentence gives!
He lives, He lives, who once was dead;
He lives, my everlasting Head.

He lives triumphant from the grave,
He lives eternally to save,
He lives all-glorious in the sky,
He lives exalted there on high.

He lives to bless me with His love,
He lives to plead for me above,
He lives my hungry soul to feed,
He lives to help in time of need.

He lives to grant me rich supply,
He lives to guide me with His eye,
He lives to comfort me when faint,
He live to hear my soul's complaint.

He lives to silence all my fears,
He lives to wipe away my tears,
He lives to calm my troubled heart,
He lives all blessings to impart.

He lives, my kind, wise, heav'nly Friend,
He lives and loves me to the end;
He lives, and while He lives, I'll sing;
He lives, my Prophet, Priest, and King.

He lives and grants me daily breath;
He lives and I shall conquer death;
He lives my mansion to prepare;
He lives to bring me safely there.

He lives, all glory to His name!
He lives, my Jesus, still the same.
Oh, the sweet joy this sentence gives,
"I know that my Redeemer lives!"

Authorship

"I Know That My Redeemer Lives," a well-known hymn expressing confidence in the resurrection and redemption, was written by an 18th-century English Baptist minister Samuel Medley. Born in 1738, Medley's life unfolded during a time when evangelical fervour was sweeping through England. His hymnody reflects not only his theological convictions but also the vibrant religious atmosphere of the 18th century.

Samuel Medley's early life took an unexpected turn when, as a young man, he joined the Royal Navy. It was during his naval service that a life-altering event occurred - he was severely wounded in battle. This experience led him to reevaluate his priorities and his eventual conversion to Christianity. After leaving the Royal Navy Medley felt a calling to the ministry and became a Baptist pastor.

"I Know That My Redeemer Lives" emerged from Medley's personal reflections on his faith journey and the assurance he found in the redemptive work of Christ. The hymn exudes an intense sense of gratitude and confidence in the risen Redeemer. Medley's work became highly regarded for its emotional depth and evangelical fervour, contributing to the rich tradition of Baptist hymnody in the 18th century.

In the broader context of the 18th century, England was experiencing the effects of the Evangelical Revival led by figures such as John Wesley and George Whitefield. This religious awakening influenced Medley's ministry and hymn writing, and "I Know That My Redeemer Lives" became a hymn that resonated not only with his congregation but also with Christians across denominational lines. Samuel Medley's life story, marked by personal transformation and a dedication to proclaiming the Christian message, adds a poignant layer of significance to this timeless hymn.

The story within the hymn

"I Know That My Redeemer Lives" shares a confident and personal narrative affirming the belief in the living Redeemer. Each verse is a proclamation of faith, where the lyrics transform into a resolute declaration of the assurance found in the Redeemer's life.

The verses are a journey of conviction, prompting us to express unwavering confidence in the resurrected Saviour. They are a celebration of the living Redeemer who brings hope, redemption and eternal life.

Narrative: This personal hymn tells the story of unwavering faith, declaring confidence in the Redeemer who lives. It's a hymn that emotionally describes the story of assurance in the reality of resurrection and the living Redeemer.

Musical Tone: The music, with its steady and affirming tones, creates a feeling of surety and assurance to encourage a steadfast faith in the Redeemer.

Devotional

Living Redeemer, with confidence, we declare that you are alive. As we rest in the assurance of your life, may our faith be strengthened, and may we live in the freedom and joy that comes from knowing you.

Romans 6:4

"We were therefore buried with him through baptism into death in order that, just as Christ was raised from the dead through the glory of the Father, we too may live a new life."

In this passage Paul illustrates the symbolism of baptism, connecting it to the death and resurrection of Jesus and the promise of new life.

Prayer

God, as I reflect on my baptism, I celebrate the new life I have in Christ. Thank You for the transformative power of Your resurrection.

18
Welcome, Happy Morning
Venantius Fortunatus, John Ellerton (translation)

"Welcome, happy morning!"
Age to age shall say:
"Hell today is vanquished;
Heav'n is won today!"
Lo, the dead is living,
God forevermore!
Him, their true Creator,
All his works adore.

"Welcome, happy morning!"
Age to age shall say:
"Hell today is vanquished;
Heav'n is won today!"

Maker and Redeemer,
Life and health of all,
God from heav'n beholding
Human nature's fall,
Of the Father's Godhead
You, the only Son,
Mankind to deliver
Manhood did put on.

"Welcome, happy morning!"
Age to age shall say:
"Hell today is vanquished;
Heav'n is won today!"

Source of all things living,
You came down to die,
Plumbed the depths of hell
To raise us up on high.
Come, then, true and faithful,
Come fulfill your word;
This is our third morning -
Rise, O buried Lord.

"Welcome, happy morning!"
Age to age shall say:
"Hell today is vanquished;
Heav'n is won today!"

Free the souls long prisoned,
Bound with Satan's chain;
All that now is fallen
Raise to life again.
Show your face in brightness;
Shine in ev'ry land
As in Eden's garden
When the world began.

"Welcome, happy morning!"
Age to age shall say:
"Hell today is vanquished;
Heav'n is won today!"

Authorship

Venantius Fortunatus, born in the late 6th century in Italy, was known for his Latin poetry and hymns. While the original Latin text of "Welcome, Happy Morning" is ascribed to him, it was translated into English by John Ellerton in the 19th century. Fortunatus lived during a time when the Western Christian Church was still emerging from the cultural and political transformations of the post-Roman period. His hymns, with their vivid imagery and theological depth, played in important part in the evolution of early Christian hymnody.

John Ellerton, born in 1826, was a Victorian-era Anglican clergyman and hymn writer. Living in a period marked by social and industrial changes, Ellerton was part of the Oxford Movement, a 19th-century revival within the Anglican Church that sought to bring about a return to more traditional and liturgical practices. Ellerton's translation of "Welcome, Happy Morning" was influenced by this movement, reflecting a renewed interest in the hymns of early Christian writers like Fortunatus.

The hymn itself celebrates the joy and victory of Easter morning, proclaiming the resurrection of Jesus Christ. "Welcome, Happy Morning" has become a notable addition to Victorian hymnals, embodying the spirit of resurrection and the theological richness associated with Easter. Its enduring popularity underscores its ability to resonate with worshipers across centuries and cultural contexts. The collaborative effort of Fortunatus and Ellerton encapsulates the hymn's journey through time and its impact on Christian worship traditions.

The story within the hymn

"Welcome, Happy Morning" is an expression of joyful gratitude for the resurrection on Easter morning, inviting us to enter into the festive atmosphere of resurrection day. The hymn is a celebration of new beginnings, through a collective expression of joy and praise. The story is a journey of jubilation, prompting us to rejoice in the transformative power of Easter. A sense of gladness evolves through each verse, with the herald of a new day of eternal hope through the risen Christ.

The hymn opens with an exclamation of the happy morning heralding the vanquishing of hell and the conquering of heaven, emphasising the resurrection of the dead and the everlasting presence of God as the true Creator. The lyrics then describe Christ as both Maker and Redeemer, portraying His divine origin and the embodiment of human nature to deliver mankind. The repetition of the refrain reinforces the continuous celebration across ages of Christ's triumph over hell and the securing of heaven.

The third verse acknowledges Christ as the source of all life, emphasising His descent to die and His resurrection, symbolised by rising from the depths of hell. It calls for Christ to fulfil His promise and rise as the buried Lord on this third morning, echoing the theme of resurrection and renewal.

The final highlight is the liberation of souls long imprisoned by Satan's chain, and the restoration of fallen creation to life. It calls for Christ's radiant presence to shine across the world, akin to the splendour of Eden's garden at the beginning of creation.

Through its lyrical story "Welcome, Happy Morning!" weaves a narrative of Christ's triumphant victory over death, His role as both Creator and Redeemer, and the promise of renewal and eternal life for all. The repeated refrain reinforces the timeless celebration of this profound message across the ages.

Narrative: This hymn tells the story of Easter morning, capturing the jubilant atmosphere surrounding the risen Christ with a joyous welcome to a new day of triumph and victory over the grave.

Musical Tone: Throughout the music a mood of festive jubilation and joy is created with lively melodies emphasising and enhancing the celebration of Easter.

Devotional

Lord of all mornings, we welcome this happy morning with hearts full of gratitude. May the joy of Easter permeate our lives, bringing renewed hope, happiness, and a deeper connection to your resurrection power.

Acts 2:24

"But God raised him from the dead, freeing him from the agony of death, because it was impossible for death to keep its hold on him."

In this verse Peter proclaims that God raised Jesus from the dead, breaking the power of death.

Prayer

Gracious God, thank You for overcoming death through the resurrection of Jesus. May I live in the freedom and hope of Your victory.

19
Alleluia, Sing to Jesus
William Chatterton Dix

Alleluia! Sing to Jesus;
His the scepter, His the throne.
Alleluia! His the triumph,
His the victory alone.
Hark! The songs of peaceful Zion
Thunder like a mighty flood:
"Jesus out of every nation
Has redeemed us by His blood."

Alleluia! Not as orphans
Are we left in sorrow now.
Alleluia! He is near us;
Faith believes, nor questions how.
Tho' the cloud from sight received Him
When the forty days were o'er,
Shall our hearts forget His promise,
"I am with you evermore"?

Alleluia! Bread of heaven,
Here on earth our food, our stay.
Alleluia! Here the sinful
Flee to You from day to day.
Intercessor, Friend of sinners,

Earth's Redeemer, hear our plea
Where the songs of all the sinless
Sweep across the crystal sea.

Authorship

William Chatterton Dix 1837–1898), an English hymn writer, wrote "Alleluia, Sing to Jesus" in the 19th century. Born in Bristol, England, in 1837, Dix lived during a period of changes across society in Victorian Britain. His hymnody reflects both the challenges and hopes of his time. With an early career in business, his life took a different direction after a severe illness led to a spiritual awakening. Following his recovery, Dix dedicated himself to writing hymns that conveyed Christian truths in a meaningful and accessible way. "Alleluia, Sing to Jesus" is one of his most enduring contributions to hymnody.

This joyful hymn captures the essence of worship, focusing on the presence of Christ in the Eucharist and expressing praise throughout the word "Alleluia." Dix's composition blends theological richness with poetic beauty. The context of Victorian England, with its industrialisation and societal challenges, influenced his writing by providing a backdrop of both spiritual longing and steadfast hope. "Alleluia, Sing to Jesus" is a globally popular hymn, particularly through its ability to articulate the Christian faith in a way that resonates with the challenges and aspirations of his era. Dix's life and hymnody continue to impact congregations, offering a timeless expression of praise and devotion.

The story within the hymn

"Alleluia, Sing to Jesus" is often sung during the Easter season and focuses on the glory of Christ's exaltation. It is a joyful expression of praise, celebrating the ascended Lord and King through its verses inviting worshipers to enter into a reverent atmosphere of adoration. The hymn is a musical proclamation of Christ's exaltation and collective expression of homage and praise. It is a majestic and reverent testament to the glorious narrative of Christ's ascension and His everlasting sovereignty.

The hymn begins with a joyous call to worship, prompting us to lift praises to Jesus. It highlights His' authority as symbolised by the sceptre and ultimate rule represented by the throne. The ensuing line rejoices in Jesus' personal triumph and victory, with "Alleluia" expressing an overarching sentiment of joy and praise. The hymn then paints a vivid image of a peaceful community of believers, their songs resonating like a mighty flood, symbolising a powerful and echoing sound. The final line underscores the universal impact of Jesus' sacrifice, emphasising His redemption extending to every nation and corner of the world through the shedding of His blood on the cross.

The lyrics then reassure us that we are not left alone in sorrow, using the poignant metaphor of orphans to convey a sense of care and guidance. It then declares that, despite not physically seeing Jesus, we have faith that He is near, encouraging trust without the need for exhaustive explanations. The reference to the cloud receiving Him after forty days alludes to the biblical narrative of Jesus' ascension into heaven post-resurrection. The narrative sets a questioning tone, pondering whether our hearts will forget Jesus' enduring promise to be with us always.

Finally, the hymn beautifully describes Jesus as the "Bread of Heaven," emphasising His role as the spiritual sustenance for earthly lives. It acknowledges that sinners find refuge in Jesus, turning to Him for forgiveness and assistance daily. Describing Jesus as the Intercessor, Friend of sinners, and the Redeemer of the earth, this verse articulates a plea for His intervention. The final line paints a vivid picture of a heavenly scene, imagining sinless beings singing across a crystal sea, symbolising an environment of beauty and purity.

Narrative: The verses of this hymn construct a narrative that spans reassurance, faith, questioning, and a profound depiction of Jesus as the spiritual sustenance and redeemer.

Musical Tone: The music, with its majestic and reverent tones, creates a tone of exalted worship. The harmonies and dynamics convey a mood of reverence, enhancing the narrative of alleluias sung to the exalted Jesus.

Devotional

King of Glory, as we sing alleluias to Jesus, may our worship rise like sweet incense before you. May our praises be a pleasing offering, reflecting our love and adoration for the ascended Lord and King.

Mark 16:6

"Don't be alarmed,' he said. 'You are looking for Jesus the Nazarene, who was crucified. He has risen! He is not here. See the place where they laid him.'"

An angel announces Jesus' resurrection to the women, bringing a message of hope and assurance.

Prayer

Lord, like the women at the tomb, I rejoice in the news of Your resurrection. Fill my heart with the certainty of Your triumph over death."

20
Low in the Grave He Lay
Robert Lowry

Low in the grave He lay,
Jesus, my Saviour,
Waiting the coming day,
Jesus, my Lord!

Up from the grave He arose,
With a mighty triumph o'er His foes;
He arose a Victor from the dark domain,
And He lives forever, with His saints to reign.
He arose! He arose!
Hallelujah! Christ arose!

Vainly they watch His bed,
Jesus, my Saviour;
Vainly they seal the dead,
Jesus, my Lord!

Up from the grave He arose,
With a mighty triumph o'er His foes;
He arose a Victor from the dark domain,
And He lives forever, with His saints to reign.
He arose! He arose!
Hallelujah! Christ arose!

Death cannot keep his prey,
Jesus, my Saviour;
He tore the bars away,
Jesus, my Lord!

Up from the grave He arose,
With a mighty triumph o'er His foes;
He arose a Victor from the dark domain,
And He lives forever, with His saints to reign.
He arose! He arose!
Hallelujah! Christ arose!

Authorship

"Low in the Grave He Lay" was composed by Robert Lowry, an influential American Baptist minister and hymn writer who lived in the 19th century. Born in 1826 in Philadelphia, Pennsylvania, his life was characterised by a deep commitment to Christian ministry and music. He served as a pastor in various Baptist churches, contributing to the spiritual life of congregations. Lowry's hymns, including "Low in the Grave He Lay," often conveyed a sense of Christian hope and assurance in the face of life's challenges.

This hymn reflects Lowry's theology and his desire to communicate the profound truths of the Christian faith in a way that resonated with congregations. The lyrics vividly depict the events of Christ's burial and resurrection, celebrating the redemptive work of the Savior. Lowry's composition is known for its simplicity and emotional impact, making it accessible to a wide range of worshippers.

In the broader context of 19th-century America, Lowry's hymnody emerged during a period of significant social and cultural changes. The hymn resonated with a society grappling with the aftermath of the Civil War and undergoing rapid industrialisation. "Low in the Grave He Lay" became a comforting and uplifting hymn, providing a musical expression of Christian faith amid the complexities of the time. Robert Lowry's dual role as a minister and hymnist highlights his dedication to conveying the timeless message of hope through his musical contributions.

The story within the hymn

"Low in the Grave He Lay" reflects on the burial of Jesus and the anticipation of the resurrection, inviting us to enter into the solemn atmosphere of the tomb. The hymn is an expression of the hope and expectation tied to the empty grave, allowing us to join in a collective reflection on the redemptive significance of Easter. It is a jubilant hymn telling the story of Jesus' resurrection, celebrating the triumph over death and the grave.

The hymn begins by depicting Jesus in the grave, awaiting the dawn of a new day as the Saviour. The imagery sets the scene for the miraculous event to follow. The chorus refrain exclaims the joyous news of Jesus rising from the grave with a mighty triumph over His foes. The vivid language conveys the victory of Christ over the dark domain of death, emphasising that He not only arose, but lives forever, ready to reign with His saints. The repeated refrain of "He arose! He arose! Hallelujah! Christ arose!" echoes the excitement of this resurrection proclamation. Acknowledging the futile efforts of those who tried to guard Jesus' burial site, the hymn emphasises the futility of sealing the dead when faced with the power of the resurrected Lord.

The second verse mirrors the first, reinforcing the narrative of the risen Christ. The final verse triumphantly declares that death cannot retain its hold on Jesus, the Saviour. The bars that symbolise the grip of death are torn away, signifying the ultimate victory over mortality. The chorus resounds again, proclaiming the everlasting life and reign of Christ with His saints.

"Low in the Grave He Lay" is a vibrant expression of the Christian faith, rejoicing in the resurrection of Jesus and the hope it brings to believers. The hymn encapsulates the central message of Easter – the triumph of life over death through the resurrection of Christ.

Narrative: The verses tell the story of Jesus' burial and the anticipation of resurrection. It's a hymn that tells the story of the temporary state of Christ in the grave, leading to the triumphant moment of rising.

Musical Tone: The music, with contemplative and hopeful melodies, creates a tone of joyful anticipation. The harmonies convey a mood of expectation, enhancing the moments of temporary rest before the resurrection.

Devotional

Dear Lord, reflect on the moment when you lay low in the grave, and we anticipate the joy of your resurrection. As we await the dawning of Easter morning, may our hearts be filled with hope and expectation.

Philippians 3:20-21

"But our citizenship is in heaven. And we eagerly await a Saviour from there, the Lord Jesus Christ, who, by the power that enables him to bring everything under his control, will transform our lowly bodies so that they will be like his glorious body."

Paul describes believers as citizens of heaven, anticipating the day when Jesus will transform our bodies to be like His.

Prayer

Jesus, I eagerly await the day of transformation. Thank You for the hope of resurrection and the promise of being with You forever.

21
All Glory, Laud, and Honour
Theodulf of Orleans, John Mason Neale (translation)

All glory, laud, and honour
To you, Redeemer, King,
To whom the lips of children
Made sweet hosannas ring.
You are the King of Israel
And David's royal Son,
Now in the Lord's name coming,
The King and Blessed One.

The company of angels
Is praising you on high;
And we with all creation
In chorus make reply.
The people of the Hebrews
With palms before you went;
Our praise and prayer and anthems
Before you we present.

To you before your passion
They sang their hymns of praise;
To you, now high exalted,
Our melody we raise.
As you received their praises,

> Accept the prayers we bring,
> For you delight in goodness,
> O good and gracious King!

Authorship

"All Glory, Laud, and Honor" is a hymn with ancient roots attributed to Theodulf of Orleans, a medieval bishop and poet who lived in the 9th century. The hymn's enduring popularity is in part due to the translation into English by John Mason Neale, a 19th-century Anglican clergyman and hymn writer. Both figures contributed to the hymn's rich history, connecting the ancient Christian tradition with the worship practices of the Victorian era.

Theodulf of Orleans, born in Spain around 750, served as Bishop of Orleans during the Carolingian Empire. A scholar and poet, Theodulf was known for his contributions to the Carolingian Renaissance, a revival of learning and culture under the rule of Charlemagne. "All Glory, Laud, and Honor" is believed to have been written by Theodulf as an expression of praise for Christ during the celebration of Palm Sunday.

John Mason Neale, born in 1818, was a 19th-century Anglican clergyman known for his translations of ancient hymns and his role in the Oxford Movement. Living during the Victorian era, Neale sought to reintroduce medieval hymns and liturgical practices into Anglican worship. His translation of "All Glory, Laud, and Honor" preserved the hymn's religious depth and poetic beauty in English, contributing to a revival of interest in ancient Christian traditions.

The hymn itself, a triumphant procession celebrating Christ's entry into Jerusalem, carries both the theological richness of Theodulf's original composition and the Victorian-era revivalist spirit fostered by Neale. "All Glory, Laud, and Honor" stands as a bridge connecting centuries of worship, highlighting the contributions of both Theodulf and John Mason Neale to the rich variations of Christian hymnody.

The story within the hymn

"All Glory, Laud, and Honour" is often used on Palm Sunday as a proclamation to celebrate Christ as King, inviting worshippers to join in a regal procession by waving palm branches and acknowledging the triumphant entry of the King. The verses tell the story of praising and honouring Jesus Christ as the Redeemer and King. It begins by describing how children's voices joyfully sang praises to Jesus, recognising Him as the King of Israel and the royal Son of David.

The image is painted of Jesus arriving in the Lord's name, acknowledged as the Blessed One. The lyrics then portray a heavenly scene where angels praise Jesus, and all of creation joins in to respond to this divine acknowledgment. The mention of the people of the Hebrews with palms signifies the historical event of Jesus' triumphant entry, and the hymn presents our contemporary praises, prayers, and anthems as offerings before the King.

The story within the hymn also take us back to a time before Jesus' suffering, highlighting hymns of praise that were sung in anticipation of His arrival. Now, elevated and exalted, Jesus is the recipient of our melodies and prayers. The hymn emphasises Jesus' goodness and graciousness, appealing to Him as a delighted and benevolent King who takes joy in goodness.

In simpler terms, "All Glory, Laud, and Honour" tells the story of everyone, including children and angels, praising and honouring Jesus as a triumphant and gracious King and Redeemer.

Narrative: The verses recount Jesus' entry into Jerusalem, capturing the jubilant atmosphere of praise from the crowds. It's a hymn that tells the story of honouring Christ as King, laying palm branches before Him in acknowledgment of His majesty.

Musical Tone: With celebratory and majestic melodies the music creates a tone of triumphant praise and exuberant adoration.

Devotional

King of Kings, as we journey through Palm Sunday, may our hearts be attuned to the triumphal entry of Jesus. Hosanna in the highest, our King has come!

John 20:29

"Then Jesus told him, 'Because you have seen me, you have believed; blessed are those who have not seen and yet have believed.'"

Jesus speaks to Thomas telling him the importance of faith without relying on visual proof and acknowledging the special blessing for those who trust without direct observation.

Prayer

Lord, I believe in Your resurrection, even though I haven't seen. Increase my faith and help me trust in Your life-giving power.

22
Crown Him with Many Crowns
Matthew Bridges and Godfrey Thring

Crown him with many crowns,
The Lamb upon his throne.
Hark! how the heavenly anthem drowns
All music but its own.
Awake, my soul, and sing
Of him who died for thee,
And hail him as thy matchless king
Through all eternity.

Crown him the Lord of life,
Who triumphed o'er the grave,
And rose victorious in the strife
For those he came to save;
His glories now we sing
Who died and rose on high,
Who died eternal life to bring,
And lives that death may die.

Crown him the Lord of love;
Behold his hands and side,
Rich wounds, yet visible above,
In beauty glorified;
No angels in the sky

> Can fully bear that sight,
> But downward bends their burning eye
> At mysteries so bright.
>
> Crown him the Lord of years,
> The potentate of time,
> Creator of the rolling spheres,
> Ineffably sublime.
> All hail, Redeemer, hail!
> For thou hast died for me;
> Thy praise shall never, never fail
> Throughout eternity.

Authorship

"Crown Him with Many Crowns" is a hymn with collaborative authorship attributed to Matthew Bridges and Godfrey Thring, both 19th-century hymn writers. It is a notable example of their joint effort in creating a powerful and majestic expression of worship.

Matthew Bridges, born in 1800, was an English poet and hymn writer. Initially, he was a member of the Anglican Church but later converted to Roman Catholicism. "Crown Him with Many Crowns" was originally published in his hymn collection titled "The Passion of Jesus," reflecting his deep devotion to Christ and the liturgical traditions of the Catholic Church.

Godfrey Thring, born in 1823, was an Anglican clergyman and prolific hymn writer. Living during the Victorian era, Thring contributed significantly to hymnody, seeking to provide congregations with meaningful expressions of faith. His collaboration with Bridges on "Crown Him with Many Crowns" showcased their shared commitment to conveying the grandeur and majesty of Christ in worship. The hymn itself is a celebration of the multifaceted glory of Christ, drawing on biblical imagery and themes from the Book of Revelation. The collaborative effort of Bridges and Thring resulted in a hymn that has transcended denominational boundaries and become a cherished part of Christian worship globally.

In the context of 19th-century England, societal changes, religious revivals, and a growing interest in hymnody influenced the creative endeavours of writers like Bridges and Thring. "Crown Him with Many Crowns" remains a powerful testament to their collaborative genius, blending theological depth with poetic beauty to create a hymn that continues to inspire worship across denominations and generations.

The story within the hymn

The hymn "Crown Him with Many Crowns" is an expression of adoration and worship for Jesus Christ, depicting various aspects of His majesty and glory. In the first verse, the imagery of crowning Jesus with many crowns symbolises His sovereignty and lordship. The mention of the Lamb upon His throne refers to Jesus as both the sacrificial Lamb and the exalted ruler. The heavenly anthem is described as drowning out all other music, emphasising the unmatched and supreme nature of Christ. The call to the soul to sing and hail Jesus as the matchless king reflects the eternal praise and worship due to Him for His sacrificial death.

The second verse continues to exalt Jesus, recogniSing Him as the Lord of life who triumphed over the grave. The language tells the victory Jesus achieved through His resurrection and His role as the Saviour. The mention of His glories and the purpose of His death to bring eternal life further glorifies Him. The third verse focuses on Jesus as the Lord of love, pointing to the wounds on His hands and side as visible signs of His sacrificial love. The description of these wounds as rich and glorified adds a profound depth to the visual representation of Christ's love. The reference to angels bending their burning eyes at the sight reflects the awe-inspiring nature of this divine love.

The fourth verse expands the praise by acknowledging Jesus as the Lord of years, the Creator of the universe. Concluding with a triumphant declaration of praise to the Redeemer, the hymn expresses gratitude for His sacrifice and affirming that His praise will endure throughout eternity.

In summary, "Crown Him with Many Crowns" has a story that beautifully captures the multifaceted majesty and glory of Jesus Christ. It invites us to worship Him as the matchless king, triumphant Lord of life, embodiment of love, and eternal Creator.

Narrative: The verses tell the story of Christ's supreme reign, adorned with countless crowns that represent His authority and majesty. It's a hymn that narrates the story of joining the heavenly anthem in proclaiming the greatness of the crowned King.

Musical Tone: The music, with its regal and majestic tones, creates a tone of reverent exaltation, conveying a mood of awe and adoration.

Devotional

Crowned Redeemer, we lift our voices in praise, crowning you with many crowns. May our worship be a reflection of your majesty, acknowledging you as the worthy King of kings and Lord of lords.

Ephesians 1:19-20

".. and his incomparably great power for us who believe. That power is the same as the mighty strength he exerted when he raised Christ from the dead and seated him at his right hand in the heavenly realms."

In this passage Paul speaks of the immeasurable greatness of God's power, which raised Christ from the dead and seated Him at the right hand of God.

Prayer

Mighty God, thank You for the resurrection power at work in my life. May I live in the fullness of Your strength and grace.

23
Love Divine, All Loves Excelling
Charles Wesley

Love divine, all loves excelling,
Joy of heav'n to earth come down,
Fix in us Thy humble dwelling;
All Thy faithful mercies crown!
Jesus, Thou art all compassion,
Pure, unbounded love Thou art;
Visit us with Thy salvation;
Enter every trembling heart.

Breathe, O breathe Thy loving Spirit
Into every troubled breast!
Let us all in Thee inherit,
Let us find the promised rest.
Take away our love of sinning;
Alpha and Omega be;
End of faith, as its beginning,
Set our hearts at liberty.

Come, Almighty to deliver;
Let us all Thy life receive;
Suddenly return and never,
Nevermore Thy temples leave.
Thee we would be always blessing,
Serve Thee as Thy hosts above;

> Pray, and praise Thee without ceasing,
> Glory in Thy perfect love.
>
> Finish then, Thy new creation;
> Pure and spotless let us be;
> Let us see Thy great salvation
> Perfectly restored in Thee.
> Changed from glory into glory,
> Till in heav'n we take our place,
> Till we cast our crowns before Thee,
> Lost in wonder, love, and praise.

Authorship

Charles Wesley (1707–1788), one of the founders of Methodism, penned "Love Divine, All Loves Excelling" in the 18th century. This hymn is a heartfelt prayer for the transformation of the heart by God's love. It reflects on the desire for God's presence to dwell within and empower believers to attain perfection in love. See also hymn 11 "Christ the Lord Is Risen Today".

The story within the hymn

"Love Divine, All Loves Excelling" is a heartfelt hymn that serves as a sincere prayer expressing deep devotion to Jesus Christ. It starts by calling on Jesus to bring His divine love into our lives, asking for His constant presence and mercy, describing Jesus as the embodiment of joy from heaven coming down to earth. The story then acknowledges Jesus as a boundless source of compassion and love, asking Him to transform our lives. It expresses a longing for salvation and renewal, inviting Jesus into our hearts.

The words also ask the Holy Spirit to bring comfort and peace to troubled hearts, seeking freedom from the love of sin. The hymn calls on Jesus to share His life with us and expresses the hope for His lasting presence. It desires to bless and serve Jesus continually, echoing the devotion of heavenly beings. The hymn concludes with a prayer for the completion of God's new creation, aspiring to be transformed and restored by God's great salvation.

In simpler terms, "Love Divine, All Loves Excelling" is a beautiful prayer asking Jesus to fill our lives with His love, bring comfort to our troubles, and guide us on a path of spiritual growth and salvation. It expresses a deep desire to live in constant communion with Jesus, seeking His presence and grace in our lives.

Narrative: The verses narrate the story of seeking divine love, acknowledging human inadequacy, and desiring the transformative power of God's love. It's a hymn that tells the story of a soul yearning for the excellence of divine love to abound.

Musical Tone: The music, with its tender and contemplative melodies, creates a tone of earnest supplication. A mood of humility and longing evolves enhancing the meaning of the words in seeking divine love's transformative touch.

Devotional

Divine Love, as we pray for your transformative love to dwell within us, may our hearts be open to the immense power of your grace. Teach us to love as you love, with a love that surpasses all understanding.

John 20:17

"Jesus said, 'Do not hold on to me, for I have not yet ascended to the Father. Go instead to my brothers and tell them, "I am ascending to my Father and your Father, to my God and your God."'"

After His resurrection, Jesus speaks to Mary Magdalene who is the first see Him. She is instructed not to physically hold onto Him, suggesting a transition and a shift in the nature of Jesus' presence. She is then commissioned to inform the disciples about the resurrection and message of Christ's victory over death.

Prayer

Lord, help us embrace the transformative power of Your resurrection, understanding that sometimes we must let go of the familiar to usher in a new presence. May we, like Mary Magdalene, boldly share the message of Your victory over death with those around us.

24
Now Thank We All Our God
Martin Rinkart, Catherine Winkworth (translation)

Now thank we all our God
With heart and hands and voices,
Who wondrous things has done,
In whom his world rejoices;
Who from our mothers' arms
Has blessed us on our way
With countless gifts of love,
And still is ours today.

O may this bounteous God
Through all our life be near us,
With ever joyful hearts
And blessed peace to cheer us,
To keep us in his grace,
And guide us when perplexed,
And free us from all ills
Of this world in the next.

All praise and thanks to God
The Father now be given,
The Son and Spirit blest,
Who reign in highest heaven
The one eternal God,
Whom heaven and earth adore;

For thus it was, is now,
And shall be evermore.

Authorship

"Now Thank We All Our God" was originally written by Martin Rinkart, a 17th-century Lutheran pastor, and later translated into English by Catherine Winkworth, a 19th-century English translator and hymn writer. This hymn represents a beautiful intersection of historical Lutheran tradition and Victorian-era hymnody.

Martin Rinkart, born in 1586 in Germany, lived through the turbulent times of the Thirty Years' War. Despite the challenges and hardships of the war, Rinkart remained steadfast in his faith and ministry. "Now Thank We All Our God" was created as a deep expression of gratitude and trust in God amid adversity. Rinkart's life story, marked by pastoral dedication during a period of immense suffering, adds depth to the hymn's themes of thanksgiving and trust.

Catherine Winkworth, born in 1827 in London, was an accomplished translator and hymn writer. Living during the Victorian era, Winkworth was passionate about making German hymns accessible to English-speaking audiences. Her translation of "Now Thank We All Our God" was part of her broader effort to introduce German hymnody to the English-speaking world. Winkworth's translations contributed significantly to Victorian hymnody, reflecting her commitment to providing congregations with a rich repertoire of hymns that conveyed theological depth and spiritual insight.

In the context of the Thirty Years' War and the Victorian era, "Now Thank We All Our God" emerged as a timeless hymn that crosses historical and cultural boundaries. It has become a staple in worship services, symbolising gratitude and trust in God's providence. The collaborative impact of Rinkart and Winkworth showcases the enduring power of hymnody to connect different times, cultures, and traditions through expressions of faith and thanksgiving.

The story within the hymn

As a hymn of gratitude and praise to God for the wonderful things He has done, "Now Thank We All Our God" begins by expressing thanksgiving with heart, hands, and voices. The narrative beautifully acknowledges God's wondrous deeds that bring joy to the world. Highlighting the continuous blessings received from God since birth, it emphasises the countless gifts of love He bestows upon each individual.

The story within the hymn then becomes a prayer, asking for God's continued presence throughout life. It seeks God's nearness, joyful hearts, and peace to accompany us through all circumstances. There's a plea for divine guidance during moments of confusion and a request for protection from the challenges of this world and the next.

The hymn concludes with a comprehensive acknowledgment of the trinity of God as Father, Son, and Holy Spirit. It offers praise and thanks, proclaiming His reign in the highest heaven. The closing lines affirm the enduring nature of God's presence and praise, declaring that He was, is, and shall be evermore.

In simpler terms, "Now Thank We All Our God" is a hymn of appreciation, thanking God for His continuous blessings and seeking His guidance and presence in every aspect of life. It expresses gratitude for the past, seeks God's help for the present, and confidently acknowledges His eternal reign in the future.

Meaning: This hymn is a song of gratitude and thanksgiving for God's blessings expressing thankfulness for God's providence and mercy, even in times of trial.

Musical Tone: The uplifting and grateful music offers a tone of joyful thanksgiving creating a mood of appreciation and contentment to enhance the narrative of heartfelt gratitude.

Devotional

Gracious Provider, on this day of thanksgiving, we express our gratitude for your countless blessings. May our hearts overflow with thankfulness, and may our lives be a continual offering of thanks to you, our God.

1 Corinthians 15:54-55

"When the perishable has been clothed with the imperishable, and the mortal with

immortality, then the saying that is written will come true: 'Death has been swallowed up in victory.'"

In this verse Paul declares the victory over death through Christ's resurrection, proclaiming that death has been swallowed up in triumph.

Prayer

Victorious Saviour, thank You for conquering death. In the face of challenges, I rest in the assurance of Your resurrection triumph.

25
Praise to the Lord, the Almighty
Joachim Neander

Praise to the Lord, the Almighty, the King of creation!
O my soul, praise him, for he is your health and salvation!
Come, all who hear; now to his temple draw near,
Join me in glad adoration.

Praise to the Lord, above all things so wondrously reigning;
Sheltering you under his wings, and so gently sustaining!
Have you not seen all that is needful has been
Sent by his gracious ordaining?

Praise to the Lord, who will prosper your work and defend you;
Surely his goodness and mercy shall daily attend you.
Ponder anew what the Almighty can do,
If with his love he befriends you.

Praise to the Lord! O let all that is in me adore him!
All that has life and breath, come now with praises before him.
Let the Amen sound from his people again;
Gladly forever adore him.

Authorship

Joachim Neander (1650–1680), a German Reformed Church teacher, wrote the original German text of this hymn whilst the English translation by Catherine Winkworth (1827–1878) is widely used. "Praise to the Lord, the Almighty" is a hymn of worship and praise, acknowledging the greatness and sovereignty of God. It has been embraced across denominations for its exuberant celebration of God's attributes.

Joachim Neander, born in 1650, spent much of his life in the vicinity of Düsseldorf, Germany. He is known for his deep love of nature, and many of his hymns, including "Praise to the Lord, the Almighty," draw inspiration from the natural world. Neander's hymnody reflects his Reformed theological convictions and his desire to provide congregations with hymns that combine praise and doctrinal richness.

Catherine Winkworth, born in 1827, was a prolific translator who dedicated herself to making German hymns available to English-speaking audiences. Living during the Victorian era, Winkworth contributed significantly to the popularity of German hymnody in English-speaking churches. See also hymn 24, "Now Thank We All Our God."

The hymn itself is a majestic expression of praise and adoration, echoing themes found in the Psalms. Its enduring popularity in both German and English-speaking traditions attests to its universal appeal. In the context of the 17th-century Reformed Church and the 19th-century Victorian era, "Praise to the Lord, the Almighty" has become a timeless hymn that continues to inspire worshippers across denominations, reflecting the collaborative efforts of Neander and Winkworth to create a piece that transcends cultural and linguistic boundaries.

The story within the hymn

"Praise to the Lord, the Almighty" expresses deep praise and gratitude to God, acknowledging Him as the King of creation and the source of health and salvation. The call to praise throughout is extended to everyone, prompting us to come and join in joyful worship at His temple. Reverent lyrics highlight God's wonderful reign and protective care, comparing it to being sheltered under His wings. The hymn emphasises divine providence, expressing the belief that everything essential is sent according to God's gracious plan, declaring a deep trust in His guidance and provision.

The hymn speaks of God's promise to prosper and defend those who trust in Him. His goodness and mercy are expected to accompany believers each day as we are encouraged to reflect on the mighty deeds that God can accomplish when love is shared. The final call is for us all to offer praises to God, with a resounding "Amen" expressing eternal adoration. The hymn is a celebration of God's greatness, care, and the ongoing relationship between the Creator and his followers.

Narrative: The verses share a story of universal praise to the Almighty, acknowledging His reign and exalting His attributes. It's a hymn that tells the story of creation joining in a harmonious chorus of worship to the Lord.

Musical Tone: Majestic and powerful tones create a tone of reverent praise, conveying a mood of awe and adoration.

Devotional

Majestic Lord, we offer our praises to you. As we lift our voices in worship, may our praise be a fragrant offering before your throne. You are worthy of all honour, glory, and praise, now and forever. Amen.

Revelation 1:1

"I am the Living One; I was dead, and now look, I am alive for ever and ever! And I hold the keys of death and Hades."

Jesus is declaring his triumph over death and his authority over both the state of physical death and the realm of departed souls. Holding the keys to death and Hades signifies his control and power over life and the afterlife.

Prayer

Dear Lord, we celebrate Your victory over death and thank you for conquering the grave and offering us the hope of eternal life. Help us trust in Your power and embrace the promise of everlasting life through faith in You.

A joyful Easter to you!

Thank you for embarking on this spiritual journey with us through some of the most cherished and popular hymns of Easter and Lent. We appreciate the time you've invested in discovering the stories behind these timeless musical treasures.

It has been a pleasure delving into the rich histories and origins of each hymn, and we trust that this book has added depth and insight to your Easter and Lenten season. As you engage with these hymns, whether singing them with loved ones, as part of your community celebrations, or quietly reflecting on their melodies, we hope they bring a renewed sense of joy, warmth, and contemplation.

We trust that the devotional sections of this book have provided moments of reflection and inspiration. The bible passages and prayers, aligned with the themes of the hymns, offer a sanctuary for personal contemplation. As you integrate these words into your daily routine, may they bring tranquility and spiritual grounding to your days.

Our goal has been to create a space for you to not only discover the origins of these hymns but also to find solace and understanding in your daily life, fostering a deeper connection to the true significance of the Easter season. We invite you to continue this faithful journey, letting these words guide you in moments of quiet reflection and spiritual enrichment.

Thank you for allowing us to accompany you through the sacred and joyful season of Easter. In this time of traditions and we are honoured to be a part of yours. May the spirit of this holy season envelop you with peace and happiness, and may these hymns continue to inspire and comfort you.

We wish you a Blessed Easter filled with hope and renewal.

Also by Polmarron Press

Moments of Prayer. Daily devotions for women and moments with God for every season. Over 400 personal prayers and devotionals with Bible verses for faith throughout the year.

Joyful Noel. Rediscover 25 classic Christmas hymns and carols through the Advent season. With short author histories and the stories within each hymn, daily devotionals and personal prayers.

Shop both books on Amazon by scanning the QR code and through our website. Join our newsletter for book launches and free eBook promotions.

www.polmarronpress.com

Printed in Great Britain
by Amazon